...and Kov

...and Kovno wept

Waldemar Ginsburg

...and Kovno wept

Waldemar Ginsburg

Quill

...and Kovno wept

Waldemar Ginsburg

Published in Great Britain by
Quill Press
Woodlands, Main Street, Kirton,
Newark, Nottinghamshire. NG22 9LP

© 2004 Quill Press

British Library Catalogue in Publication Data
A catalogue record for this book is available from the British
Library

ISBN 0-9543001-5-7
(First published with the ISBN 1-900-381-07-9)

Design and Production: The Holocaust Centre Design Studio
Printed and bound by Biddles Ltd.

In memory of my family and community,
victims of the genocide of the Lithuanian Jews

Dedicated to my wife, Ibi,
to my children
and
my children's children

T A B L E O F C O N T E N T S

LIST OF ILLUSTRATIONS

Author's own collection

1. Waldemar, age 17, in Kaunas, 1938.

2. Waldemar on holiday with his bicycle,
   in Kulautuva, 1937.

3. Waldemar with his mother at the
   Baltic sea in Palanga.

4. The family's pre-war flat (picture taken in 1987).

5. Munich, 1946.

6. Waldemar in Munich, 1947.

7. Radio training, Munich, 1948.

8. Wedding day, 1946: Waldemar and his wife, Ibi.

9. Munich, 1948.

10. Waldemar with his wife, Ibi, 1998.

11. Waldemar and Ibi's granddaughter, Amy

Yad Vashem Archives

12. Lithuanian vegetable market.

13. Lithuanian citizens assist the Nazis in
    killing Jews in Kaunas.

United States Holocaust Memorial Museum Archives

Beth Shalom

FOREWORD

I cannot get out of my mind the image of that youthful and confident teenager waiting in line to demonstrate his acceptability to the new masters. They had asked for 'intellectuals' to volunteer to help in the city archives. Waldemar Ginsburg had everything to make life make sense. He was young, intelligent and incredibly perceptive. He spoke five languages, was enrolled as a student of architecture and looked forward to his career in his home town of Kaunas (Kovno), Lithuania. He waited in line, hoping to be among the 500 men chosen for what would certainly be a safe occupation. To his disappointment, they stopped a few men short of him and Waldemar had to go home without being appointed. The next day, all 500 were dead.

There is now a plethora of survivor accounts of the Holocaust. Many individuals, such as Waldemar Ginsburg, have chosen to share the most bitter episodes of their lives. For those of us who were not there, who have not been through such extremes of human suffering, there is an opportunity to come a little closer to that which is beyond our experience. But do not be easily fooled. Though you may read, you can be certain that understanding the physical, mental and emotional pain is something which words fail to convey. Or maybe those of us who were not there simply cannot understand the words, and what they really mean.

Waldemar Ginsburg takes us into that world with clarity and with poise. There is no rancour or bitterness as he describes the madness and the tragedy of those terrible years. Yet there is pathos throughout. It is a pathos couched in an often understated and unemotional style, but through his precise and carefully chosen words, we become increasingly aware of the devastating nature of the Nazi assault on the Jews of Lithuania. One by one, all those he loved, and who loved him, were caught up in the insanity of mass death.

For any student of the Holocaust, this vivid and accurate account of life in the Kaunas ghetto will give an indispensable insight into the treatment of the Jews in Lithuania. It is a memorial, a document and a means of learning. Through it, Waldemar Ginsburg pays tribute to his family and to his community; he also gives those of us who did not know them an opportunity to pay tribute too.

During the Nazi occupation of Lithuania, over 90 per cent of the Jewish population were murdered. Among them were the family and friends of Waldemar Ginsburg. In June 1941, on the eve of occupation, all the members of his family met to discuss what to do in response to the looming threat. Only Waldemar survived to tell this story.

Stephen D. Smith
1998

What is not acknowledged
cannot be healed

INTRODUCTION

Fifty-three years have passed since a Free French reconnaissance unit appeared on the horizon and after four years of imprisonment I was free again. But it was only after a long pause that I was able to fulfil my intention to write my memoirs. My first attempt to put pen to paper was during the heady days of the liberation euphoria, but as the scale of the Holocaust and the extent of my personal losses revealed themselves, feelings of grief, guilt and shame overwhelmed me. During this state of self-reproach, I tore up my writing.

With the passage of time, the wounds began to heal. The appearance of books, articles, television and radio programmes indicated that survivors can overcome their inhibitions and are prepared to bear witness. Books and documents about the Lithuanian Holocaust were published, providing me with information and reawakening the urge to join in.

I was also spurred on by the curiosity of my children asking difficult questions. "Why don't we have any grandparents like the other children?" "Why do you speak with a funny accent?" I was encouraged by the view that the disclosures of survivors could serve as a warning to the young generation and help to weaken the ever-present menace of racism and xenophobia. I decided to include some details of Lithuanian history in order to describe the origins of antisemitism and to explain how the pre-war obsession with totalitarian ideologies undermined liberal and democratic ideas, destabilized political and social life and became a catalyst for mass murder.

As soon as I sat down to write, I realised that my ambition exceeded my talent. To overcome my inadequate command of English and my patchy memory, I decided to adopt a simple, concise style, keep my emotions at bay and concentrate only on events which were clear in my memory.

I completed the task in 1991 and made enough copies to satisfy the demand of family and friends. A year ago, I submitted my manuscript to Stephen Smith, the director of the Beth Shalom Holocaust Memorial Centre, for appraisal; and I was delighted by his decision to edit and publish it as part of his Witness Collection.

For my wife Ibi and for me, the connection with Beth Shalom and the rapport with the Smith family was a stimulating and exciting experience. Beth Shalom became our place of pilgrimage and remembrance, as well as a venue for our speaking engagements.

We wish to thank the Smith family for adding a new dimension and a new purpose to our lives, with special thanks to Stephen for taking on the task of editing and publishing my manuscript.

Waldemar Ginsburg,
Elland, June 1998

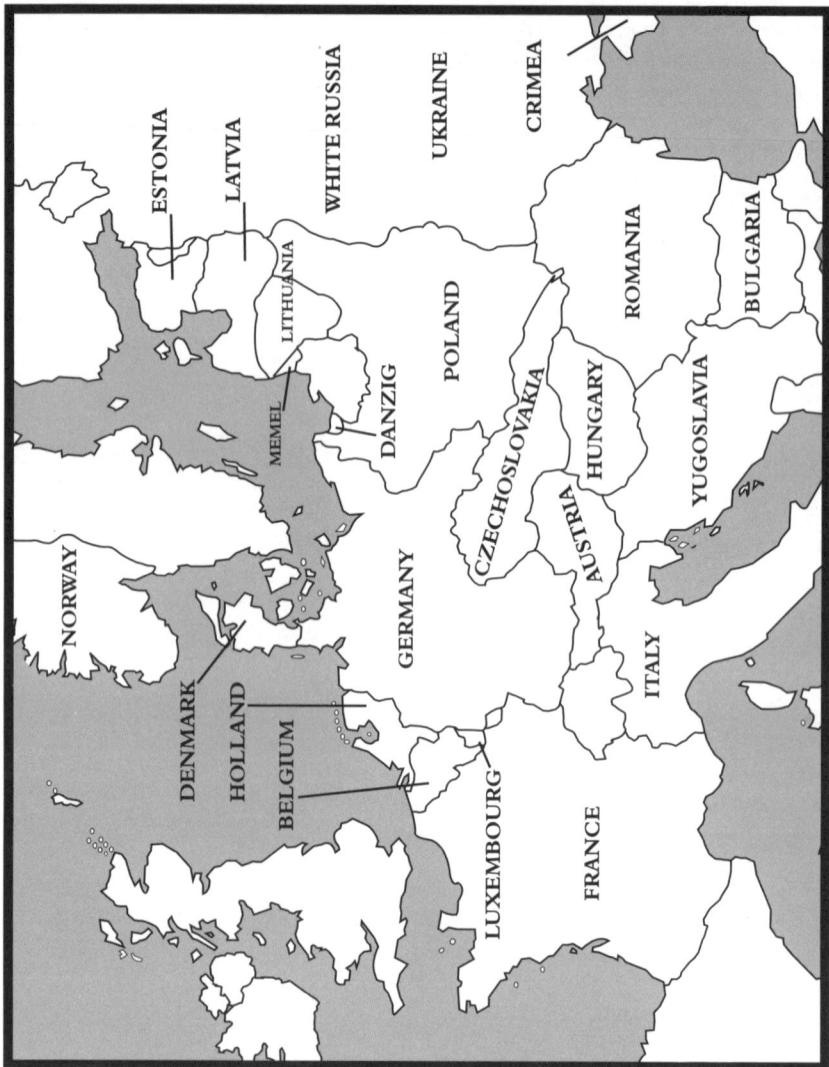

A map of pre-war east Europe

CHAPTER ONE

UNEASY PEACE

THE PRE-WAR YEARS

My Country, My Home

It was my country and my home. Now it is only a memory in my mind. It is the place where I learned about life. It is the place where I felt at home among my people. Today, I still feel a part of it, and yet it remains only a part of my past.

Lithuania, a small Baltic country in eastern Europe, has recently regained its independence after being a member of the Union of Soviet Socialist Republics for 48 years. Lithuanians are still enjoying being free of foreign domination for the second time this century. However, in the 14th and 15th centuries, it was large and powerful, ruling a territory stretching from the Baltic to the Black Sea from its capital city, Vilnius. It is difficult now to understand Lithuania as a European superpower, but for a period it was just that. At the end of the 14th century, a union with its southern neighbour, Poland, was initially of benefit to both countries. One of the more significant moments in those years of glory took place in 1410. Vytautas the Great, the Grand Duke and Viceroy of Lithuania, and his cousin Jogeilo, King of Poland, defeated the might of the German Knights of the Cross and stopped German expansion eastwards.

After the death of Vytautas the Great in 1430, the emerging

power of Muscovy began to assert its strength and wars began to go wrong. Large eastern provinces were lost. First Novgorod and Twer, then Smolensk. An appeal for Polish help was granted, but on condition of a full union between the two countries and the ceding to Poland of the provinces of Kiev and Volynia. This was known as the Union of Lublin in 1569. This union, which was dominated by Poland, did not reverse the setbacks.

The Lithuanian nobility took up the language and way of life of their decadent Polish counterparts. Eventually, the irresponsibility and corruption of the leadership in both countries became so bad that there was little resistance in 1772, when Prussia, Austria and Russia partitioned and occupied most of Poland.

In 1795, during the third and final partition, Russia took Lithuania, and the Tsar was proclaimed Grand Duke of that country. The cruel and oppressive Tsarist rule lasted for 120 years until the German armies overran the western Russian lands during the First World War. The German occupation of Lithuania did not last long. Taking advantage of the chaos resulting from the overthrow of the Tsar and the defeat of Germany, the Lithuanians proclaimed their independence in 1918.

There was an unexpected setback in 1920, when Poland broke a treaty allocating the town and the region of Vilnius – Vilna in Russian and Yiddish – to Lithuania, and annexed the capital of the newly-established state. It was a terrible blow to the Lithuanians to lose their ancient capital city, but the tiny country could not take on the might of Poland and had to move the government to a 'temporary capital' in Kaunas. In Russian and Yiddish, Kaunas was known as Kovno.

In the 1930s, this small, defenceless country of about three million people found itself sandwiched between two giant powers, the Soviet Union ruled by Stalin, and Germany, ruled by Hitler. History periodically produces such power-crazed dictators who are totally impervious to normal human feelings.

As the two tyrants grew more belligerent, it was only a matter of time before Lithuania would once again become the stamping-ground of foreign armies.

On 23 August 1939, the arch-enemies, Germany and the Soviet Union, suddenly signed a non-aggression pact, taking the whole world by surprise. There was a secret clause, found in German archives after the war, which spelled the doom of Lithuania. History was repeating itself. Poland was to be partitioned and occupied by the two superpowers; the three Baltic countries, Estonia, Latvia and Lithuania, were allocated to Russia.

On 1 September 1939, Germany invaded Poland, defeated the Polish army and annexed the western part of the country. On 17 September, the Soviet Union moved in and occupied the eastern part of Poland. Before our eyes, despite the ultimatum of France and Great Britain, Poland ceased to exist.

In June 1940, the final chapter of the Stalin-Hitler pact was enacted. The Soviet Union occupied the three Baltic States and they became members of the Union of Soviet Socialist Republics. To everybody's surprise, Stalin restored Vilnius to Lithuania, but this move did not earn him much gratitude. The opinion at the time was expressed by the saying "Vilnius belongs to us, but we belong to Russia."

Varieties of Life

During the long years of Tsarist rule, there had been an effort to Russify the populations of the occupied countries. In Lithuania, Roman Catholic worship was banned and the Russian Orthodox faith was imposed. The Latin alphabet was replaced by the Cyrillic. The population refused to accept the changes and their cultural development came to a halt. The intelligentsia had to rely for their education on German, Polish or Russian establishments of learning and hardly knew their own tongue. The language and traditions survived among the peasants in the isolation of the countryside, where Polish and Russian influences had not penetrated. When independence came, it took the emergent nation some time and an enormous effort to catch up with centuries of neglect.

The Jews played an important role in these developments by volunteering to fight for Lithuanian independence. They also joined the newly-established National Council and helped the new nation to overcome many internal and external difficulties. In 1918, at the birth of independence, the relationship between the majority and the Jewish minority population started off well. Complications only set in later.

In 1922, the Lithuanian Democratic constitution granted autonomy and parliamentary representation to all national minorities. The autonomy included full and equal civil, cultural and religious rights. The Lithuanian Jews, with their high educational level and efficient communal organisation, took advantage of the opportunities to reinforce their position as leading exponents of Jewish culture. In the capital, Kaunas, there were three Hebrew and one Yiddish full-time schools, five Yiddish newspapers, a theatre, approximately forty synagogues and some of the most prestigious yeshivas (religious schools) anywhere, to serve a Jewish community of 35,000, some 30 per cent of the total population.

In 1926, eight years after the declaration of independence, the fledgling democracy of Lithuania came to an abrupt end. The right wing National Party and the military organised a coup, grabbed power and gradually abolished the multi-party system. There were many changes, and discriminatory laws were soon introduced, curtailing the rights of the Jewish minority. The most immediate result was the removal of Jews from positions of responsibility in the government and civil service. Efforts by the opposition parties and representatives of the Jewish community to improve the situation came to nothing.

As the door to democracy was shut, the one to tragedy opened. The danger signs were slow to appear and at the time very few people appreciated the long-term implications for the minorities of the loss of representative democracy. The Jews adjusted to the new circumstances – their prominence in the professions, crafts and commerce helped them to continue to share in the growing prosperity of the country, which was due to the sound agricultural and economic policies introduced at the beginning of independence.

One of the priorities of the government was to restore the neglected native language and traditions. That was not an easy task, considering the cosmopolitan, multicultural character of Kaunas where, besides the Jewish population, there were large, well-established Polish, Russian and German minorities eager to preserve their cultural identities. Until the mid-1930s these minorities lived side by side, mixing freely with each other and with the majority population. The resulting cultural cross-fertilisation was to everybody's benefit; it broadened the outlook, introduced a variety of traditions and languages, and promoted tolerance.

Initially, the ruling National Party was controlled by the moderates, who included the President of Lithuania. Under their influence, the process of 'Lithuanianisation' was progressing at a steady pace, especially in the field of education. By the early 1930s, the changes were already apparent. Lithuanian schools were becoming more popular. They were gaining pupils at the expense of the Russian, German, Jewish and Polish schools, and the tendency to 'go native' was gaining momentum.

Europe at this time was not a place for moderation, nor a place for common sense. Open, democratic rule was in retreat and the two mutually hostile ideologies of Fascism and Communism were becoming dominant. The conflict between these totalitarian ideologies assumed the nature of a vicious circle, creating a climate of paranoia and mass hysteria.

Lithuania was not immune from the ideological fall-out. Encouraged by the successes of the Nazi party, the right-wing extremists within the ruling National Party gained ascendancy and decided to force the pace of 'Lithuanianisation'. As a result, there was an increase in xenophobia and a growing intolerance of national minorities.

The Jewish population was singled out for a campaign of hate and vilification. Although this development caused considerable anxiety, the Jews remained confident that, as loyal and law-abiding citizens, they could rely on the state for their protection.

Grandpa

I was born in Riga on 9 October 1922. My parents travelled there specifically for my birth, since they considered the hospital facilities better in Riga than in Kaunas. After two years in Kaunas, father, mother and I left Lithuania to live in France.

Before the First World War, when my father was a teenager, he made his way from Vilnius to Marseilles, signed on as a deck-hand on a merchant ship and sailed the seven seas. When he returned home and married, he found it difficult to settle down in Kaunas. He was convinced that, with his connections in Marseilles, he could find a suitable shore-based job with his old shipping firm. It did not work out. Within four years mother and father separated and at the end of the 1920s, mother and I left France, returning to Lithuania.

Father stayed in France and promised to join us at a later date. This did not happen and I never saw him again. Correspondence continued for a few more years, but when mother insisted on starting divorce proceedings, father stopped all communications and we lost touch. In Kaunas there were no close relatives from the Ginsburg family (my father's side), but my mother's family, the Stroms, was well-established and received us with open arms. Straight away I felt at home amongst its warm-hearted, close-knit members.

I was six years old when I arrived in Lithuania, but I can still remember some of my first impressions. I liked the quiet and safe streets of Kaunas, which were such a contrast to the hubbub of Marseilles, but what impressed me most was the konka. It consisted of a conventional train carriage, riding on rails and pulled by horses. A coachman with a long whip stood on the open end of the tramcar, driving the horses on. I found this combination of low and high tech irresistible and took every opportunity to drag mother onto the carriage. There I would proudly sit next to the coachman, watching him manipulate the brakes and crack the whip. Then, a few months later, to my disappointment and to the considerable relief of my mother, the konkas were replaced by buses.

I also remember the first steps of my integration into a new and unfamiliar world. Mother, who had the patience of Job, had a tough job trying to teach me the Yiddish language and trying to explain the complicated procedures of a kosher household. My grandparents were far from being zealots, but they did their best to observe the form and substance of the religious laws. Grandma concentrated on the ritual observance. Grandpa was too easygoing to be tied down with ceremonial detail, but he had a natural affinity with the moral and ethical commands of Judaism.

There were occasions which demanded a joint effort. The planning and preparation of the festival and Sabbath meals for a large family like ours was an enormous task, and it was equally shared by my grandparents. They used to remind us that it meant partaking of God's bounty and that it was an important occasion for maintaining the family bond.

The table groaned under the weight of the traditional Jewish delicacies and the bottles of wine and spirits. My favourite drink was the delicious home-made mead, a speciality of the house. It was quite potent and I loved it because of its sweet taste of honey. It made me sleepy, and well before the end of the meal I was ready for bed.

I can clearly recall the special treat I enjoyed every evening – a bedside story. Unlike a lot of kids of my age, I actually looked forward to my bedtime, which was made into a thrilling occasion by mother's knack of telling stories. She did not choose the usual children's tales. Instead, she summarised a topical news item, or a book she had read, or maybe a film she had seen. It was her skill in extracting the interesting aspects, and then reducing them to a simple, clear story which made her version of the events so fascinating for me. Later on, when I became fluent in Yiddish, Grandpa occasionally replaced my mother at my bedside. He was also an excellent raconteur and he enchanted me with his stories from the Bible.

As I grew older, he introduced me to his religious beliefs and saw me through my bar mitzvah service when I was 13. After this important initiation into Jewish adulthood, I came under the influence of my peer group, and since neither its Gentile nor its Jewish members were religious, my views changed. Full of youthful arrogance, we were searching for a rational basis for religious ideas, not realising that religion is more like a vision or an article of faith and not a suitable subject for reasoned argument. But although I had lost Grandpa's enthusiasm for the Holy Scriptures, I continued to share his pride in the historical heritage of the Lithuanian Jews, and I was enthralled by his story of their seven centuries-long presence in the country.

There was an irony in his tale of German Jews fleeing from the crusader pogroms and Christian persecution and finding refuge among the pagan tribes of Lithuania. (As late as the 14th century, the Lithuanian countryside was still pagan.) In the 14th century, their condition improved even further under the Christian rule of Grand Duke Vytautas the Great, who directed his ire towards the pagans and amity towards the Jews.

After his death, the influence of the Roman Catholic Church increased and the position of the Jews deteriorated. But unlike the clergy, who regarded Judaism as their traditional enemy, the rulers of the country viewed the Jews as loyal subjects, devoid of any political ambition, whose commercial and managerial skills could be gainfully exploited. In return, the rulers were prepared to grant the Jews important privileges, which included protection and a substantial measure of cultural autonomy. However, a successful minority is never popular. Because of their reclusiveness, different religion, language and customs, the Jews were regarded by the peasantry as a sinister, alien element. The fact that some Jews were traders, some employed as tax collectors and estate managers by grasping absentee landlords, meant that all Jews were identified with the exploitation of the peasants.

No less menacing was the endemic religious antisemitism of the population. Grandpa argued that the clergy could have used their power and influence to promote understanding and tolerance. Instead, they seemed to aggravate the situation by playing down the Jewish origin of Christianity and by emphasising the collective Jewish guilt for the crucifixion. The Jews were well aware of the hostility surrounding them, but the promise of protection gave them a sense of security.

The most significant development for Lithuanian Jewry was the granting of cultural autonomy, which enabled them to establish a thriving centre of Jewish culture renowned for its communal harmony, its extensive network of social welfare, the excellence of its yeshivas and, of course, the learning of its scholars.

It was one of these scholars, the famed Gaon of Vilna, Elijah ben Solomon (1720-1797), who unwittingly sowed the seeds of the Haskalah, the name given to the nineteenth-century Jewish Enlightenment. He took the daring step of introducing some secular learning into the yeshivas of Lithuania. His other achievement was to turn back the tide of the Hasidic movement which was spreading from Poland and threatening to undo all his new projects. As a follower of classical rabbinic Judaism, he looked upon the Hasidim as heretics. Their primitive escapist notions, mystic visions, superstitions and preoccupation with miracles, were in his eyes, an outrage, a triumph of ignorance over knowledge. It was a long and bitter struggle, but such was the prestige of the Gaon that in the end he prevailed. His educational innovations did not remain confined to Lithuanian yeshivas. Pupils from all over Europe attended these schools of religious study and they carried the acquired secular knowledge to their own countries.

I was amazed that, despite decades of coexistence, the legacy of the eighteenth-century sectarian conflict between the Orthodox Litvaks and the Hasidim was still very much in evidence during the inter-war years. Grandpa maintained that the antipathy was due to the iniquitous practices of the Hasidim. As an example, he cited their personality-worship: for the Orthodox followers of Judaism, there is no intermediary between God and man; the rabbi is no more than a wise and learned teacher. They looked upon the Hasidic tradition of elevating their so-called rebbe to near Messianic status as an act of sacrilege. Grandpa also disliked their cult of Sharaim, the left-overs from the rebbe's meal which the Hasidim believed were endowed with supernatural powers.

As Grandpa pointed out, it was not an inspiring spectacle to observe a crowd of zealots trying to snatch a bite from the rebbe's plate. Another legacy from the schism was the name-calling. The Litvaks referred to the Hasidim as mad zealots; they, in turn, called the Orthodox Tseilomkopp (crucifix-head), which is just about the most insulting epithet in the annals of Judaism.

In 1796, a year before the Gaon died, the reactionary Tsarist rule was imposed on Lithuania. The disastrous effect of its Russification drive on the cultural life of the Lithuanians was described previously.

Jews were also subjected to persecution, oppression and restrictions, including a ban on owning land and a requirement to reside only in certain designated areas, the so-called Pale of Settlement; but they were spared the pogroms which were wide-spread in Poland, Russia and the Ukraine. Life in the overcrowded ghettos and shtetls (small towns) was very grim. Grandpa was more fortunate as his village was in the countryside and the conditions were not as crowded as in the rest of the Pale. But life was still difficult.

He started off as the village milkman, then became an innkeeper in Babtai, a small town west of Kaunas. In the 45 years of his life spent under the rule of the Russian empire, he saw one Tsar succeeding another. A consistent aim of these absolute monarchs and their ruling clique was to uproot Jewish life. The head of the Holy Synod went so far as to declare that this was to be achieved partly by conversions to the Russian Orthodox faith, partly by emigration and partly by starvation.

In the meantime, the Jews became the ideal scapegoat for all the ills besetting the Tsarist system. Using their favourite slogan, "Beat the Jews, save Russia," agitators organised pogroms which served to divert the population from its miseries. At the local level, the Jews were at the mercy of Russian officials, who usually shared the views of their superiors. Fortunately, even their most fiercely antisemitic attitudes were tempered by corruption and inefficiency. There was a complete ban on Jewish self-government, but in Grandpa's village and in Babtai, the communal council continued to function as before. In the larger centres of the Pale of Settlement, the activities of the Jewish councils were more restricted, but even there the Jews managed to circumvent the ban. Despite sustained attempts to prohibit the use of Hebrew, the language of faith, and Yiddish, the everyday tongue, an outright ban never materialised, and so the Jews – the more learned section of the population – were able to continue their ancient tradition of worship and scholarship. According to Grandpa, the Lithuanian Jews took full advantage of this freedom to maintain their position as a primary centre of Jewish culture.

For Grandpa, one of the most regrettable features of life throughout the Pale was the lack of social contact with the Christian neighbours who were also suffering under the repressive Tsarist rule. A rapprochement between Jew and non-Jew was precluded by the endemic religious and economic antisemitism of the Christian population, and by the exclusive and isolationist nature of Judaism. The historical response to external hostility was to pack up and leave for greener pastures, or to close ranks and retreat to fortress Judaism. However, in the 19th century it was fortress Judaism itself which was shaken to its foundations by an unprecedented event – a surge towards secularism within the Jewish community.

The culprit was the Haskalah. As a cultural movement, it aimed to modernise the thoughts and attitudes of the Jews of the Pale of Settlement, and it was so effective that in many places it reduced Orthodox Judaism to minority status. Despite borrowing its ideas from the western Enlightenment, it was completely ethnocentric; its outlook and rich literature were rooted in Jewish history and tradition, in the two languages of the Pale – Hebrew and Yiddish – and in the spiritual values of Judaism.

The shock was caused by Haskalah's claim that the obsessive preoccupation with religious observance and ritual was exacerbating the backwardness and misery of ghetto life and detracting from the core values of Judaism, which were contained within its spiritual message of compassion, tolerance, decency, humility and integrity in the personal and public life of individuals.

In the second half of the 19th century, when Grandpa was born, the Haskalah culture was in full bloom. The Lithuanian Jews with their intellectual tradition were well-placed to play an important role in its development. Although Grandpa was fond of the mould-breaking new prose, poetry and plays, and admired the talent of the writers, he was perturbed by their secular bias. He was convinced that throughout centuries of dispersal and persecution, it was rabbinic Judaism which had assured Jewish survival, and he feared that the drive towards secularisation would lead to assimilation.

And indeed, just across the border, the educated, progressive German Jews were assimilating in droves, abandoning their faith as well as their Jewish identity. Grandpa expected the Jews of the

Pale to follow their example, but owing to basic differences between the two communities, their paths diverged. The western Jews were emancipated, they spoke the language of their host country and were prepared to join the rich mainstream culture.

The defection of eastern Jews from Judaism was also dramatic, but there was no rich mainstream culture to attract them. However, there was the Haskalah, the humanistic Jewish movement, designed to provide the defector with a spiritual home within his own familiar culture, and to enable him to retain his sense of Jewish identity. Lithuania became the leading exponent of the idea that Jewish identity is not necessarily bound up with religious belief, and it was a testimony to the tolerance of Lithuanian Jews that despite the diversity of views, the community remained intact.

Grandpa's attitude towards religion seemed somewhat puzzling. Some of his remarks, witticisms and critical comments regarding religious practices were not quite becoming for an Orthodox Jew. On some occasions he seemed to be echoing the views of the Haskalah modernisers and I wondered to what extent he had been influenced by them. For instance, they argued that the reliance of religious Jews on the power of prayer and the appearance of the Messiah to solve their problems was leading to stagnation. Instead, the Jews must break out of their self-imposed isolation and start shaping their own destiny by participating in the social and political life of society at large. This was a challenge to traditional thought, yet Grandpa expressed similar sentiments, albeit in a modified form.

Another of his sentiments was expressed in this phrase, "If the pious Jews would pay as much attention to the spiritual values of Judaism as they pay to the smallest detail of ritual observance, they would be saints."

His support for the Zionist cause and intense curiosity about secular knowledge was also a challenge to the views of the religious establishment. They insisted that the Jews must wait for the Messiah to lead them to the promised land, and they feared that curiosity about secular matters could diminish the ardour of biblical study.

Quite often, on arrival home from school, instead of going out to play, I had to sit down and answer Grandpa's questions, which sometimes included the unmentionable subjects of prehistory and evolution. According to the literal interpretation of the Bible, the world was created less than 5,800 years ago, the equivalent to 3761 BCE. Taking this understanding of historical time, prehistory, evolution, the Ice Age, the Neolithic Age and so forth did not exist. He sat in silence, intensely listening to my explanations, but I knew that, no matter how hard he tried, he would not be able to reconcile revealed truth with scientific truth.

In 1915 the German army occupied Lithuania and 120 years of Tsarist rule was at an end. The Commander in Chief, General Ludendorff, issued a proclamation in Yiddish explaining that he had come to liberate the Jews from the Russian yoke. But for 52,000 Jews, including Grandpa, Grandma and their family, it was too late. Having decided that they constituted a danger to their empire, the Russian government had them deported into the depths of Russia. Taking advantage of the turmoil after the First World War, the family embarked on the perilous trek home in 1919. When they arrived in Lithuania, they were destitute. It was only after some years of considerable hardship that they managed to establish their small off-licence shop to earn a steady income.

Their children, three boys and two girls, were brought up in a humble but caring and stable environment, which included all the values of Orthodox Judaism. Despite their religious background, they were seduced by the modern, outward-looking ideas, now firmly established within the Jewish community, which were starting to replace some of the older, more exclusive, inward-looking ways of traditional Judaism.

After the blood-letting of World War One, the promises of a new world order and a future without strife were irresistible to a lot of people. One striking feature of the inter-war years was the proliferation of myths, dogmas and ideologies, and the obsessive belief in them. Another was that the members of the tiny Communist Party were the real fanatics and not the religious Jews. More than half of the community considered themselves religious, but except for a minority of fundamentalists, it was either a 'cafeteria-type' Judaism (picking what one likes and ignoring the rest) or a moderate, temperate Judaism, similar to Grandpa's.

The beliefs within our family, which were prevalent among the educated section of the community, were mainly based on the ideas of secular western humanism, on the romantic notions of a progressive humanity and the perfectibility of man.

The diverse and clashing views could have pulled the community apart, but, as in the 19th century, the tradition of tolerance, the ubiquitous nature of Yiddish culture and the sense of Jewish identity ensured its survival. Our family was a good example of this tolerant attitude. Despite my grandparents' disappointment with the secular views of their children, there was no rift within the family and mutual affection prevailed.

These predominant traits, which also included generosity, kindliness and patience, made the family so pleasant to live with. They also seemed to me to be drawbacks in the struggle for existence, especially since they were compounded by a dislike of confrontation, a lack of assertiveness and an implicit trusting nature. I was wondering how they managed to get on in a world which, in my opinion, was rigged in favour of the unscrupulous. I soon realised that there were compensating traits, which I failed to take into account – the high level of education and literacy, and the propensity for hard work. By being outspoken, articulate and steadfast, they made up for the lack of push and assertiveness.

As to the dislike of confrontation, that too could be overcome, but only under the impetus of extreme provocation. On the rare occasions when the accumulated frustrations and pressures became unbearable, they would be relieved by a short outburst of temper. It would be gone as quickly as it began, but because it was unexpected and out of character, it was very effective.

Shortly after we arrived in Kaunas, my grandparents retired and made us an offer to move in with them. This enabled mother to take a full-time accountancy job. It was an indication of her determination to be independent, of her sense of pride and willpower. Even after her re-marriage, she insisted on keeping the job. She was a real chip off the old block, maybe not so easy-going as Grandpa, but equally generous, patient and tolerant.

Being the only child in a household of three devoted grown-ups was bound to affect my progress and outlook. I was a late developer, too immature and self-absorbed to appreciate my good fortune. Cocooned as I was in my little comfortable world, I took the love and dedication of my family for granted. Besides, most of the youngsters around me, my friends and relatives, also led a sheltered life similar to mine, so I had no yardstick for measuring my circumstances.

On occasions, when I overstepped the mark, the worst I could expect was a quiet but very effective telling-off by my mother. She did not bully, nor even raise her voice, but there was an authority, an inner conviction in her reproach which affected me deeply and helped me to keep on the right path.

My most vivid memories are of the long summer holidays, lasting a full three months. At the end of May, my grandparents would move lock, stock and barrel to a rented dacha on the shores of the Nemunas, the main river of Lithuania.

The dacha was usually a wooden bungalow with a large covered verandah situated amid the shady pine forests which extended right to the edge of the sandy riverside beaches. It was the ideal place for long forest walks, for messing around in boats, for swimming or sunbathing. Later in the summer, at the start of the official holidays, it would become crowded. Not only family members, but also friends and acquaintances, would arrive by paddle-steamer and all would be made equally welcome.

I preferred to cycle to the resorts. Having my bicycle handy enabled me to go for rides in the countryside, to visit other holiday places and to see my friends and relatives. One of our favourite destinations was Palanga, a beautiful resort on the Baltic sea. The beaches of fine golden sand stretched for miles, flanked by row after row of sheltering dunes. Further south there was another place of outstanding beauty – the Neringa. It was a narrow strip of land separating a large bay from the Baltic sea. The unique feature of this spit was a long chain of large hills made entirely of sand, heaped up high by the prevailing winds.

From the top of those hills, the views were truly breath-taking: on the western side, the foaming sea and its long beaches and dunes, on the eastern side the large expanse of the bay, and on the distant horizon the faint outline of the estuary of the river Nemunas. In between, nestling amongst the trees of the pine forests, were small, brightly painted summer cottages, and further south towards the east Prussian border, there was a nature reserve for the protection of the elk. The animals were very shy, and elk-spotting was a challenging and popular activity. Not far from the sanctuary there was a flying school, where I learned to fly gliders. The Neringa was my favourite holiday spot; nothing could compare with the enchantment of the fairy tale ambience of the place, nor with the thrill of gliding above the tall sandy hills.

At the beginning of September, the long holiday season was over; it was time for the family to head for home and for me to start school.

The other long break from school was in winter. The temperature stayed below freezing throughout, and the snow and ice cover lasted until early spring. It was an opportunity to engage in various winter activities. My favourite sport was skating, but we had no all-year indoor rinks. We had to wait for winter, when any piece of level ground could be flooded, loud-speakers and lighting could be installed and we could skate all evening to the accompaniment of cheerful music. The compacted icy surface made motorised traffic dangerous, so the streets were full of horse-drawn sledges filling the air with the tinkle of tiny bells. On fine days, the hillsides were packed with children, tobogganing, building snowmen and throwing snowballs.

In the early spring, at the start of the thaw, nature provided us with an awe-inspiring spectacle. As the temperature rose and cracks appeared in the thick river ice, the residents of the low-lying, unprotected part of the shore hurried to begin their flood prevention measures. The struggle of the mighty Nemunas to break the iron grip of the winter frost lasted a while. Slowly the cracks began to deepen and to widen, and then the huge mass of ice, rising steadily, tearing at the bridges and the embankment, started its noisy journey downstream. This breathtaking spectacle, watched every year by thousands of people, had a special significance: it heralded the victory of the sun over the dark winter nights and the eagerly-awaited arrival of spring. Between the crashing noises of the ice we could hear the sound of explosions. The Pioneer Corps of the army were downstream, trying to prevent an accumulation of ice by dynamiting the blocked sections. They were not always successful and a failure usually resulted in the flooding of the low-lying sections of the riverside.

Newcomers from Russia

In the mid-1930s, my mother's divorce came through and she married Samuel Garson, a recent arrival from Russia. His family originated from Lithuania; his father, Mark Garson, was the original owner of the fleet of paddle-steamers plying the river Nemunas. He and his brother Mike had been sent to St Petersburg to study civil and construction engineering. They graduated at the beginning of World War One.

As soon as the Garson brothers settled in Kaunas, a close relationship developed between them and our family. We had a lot of interests in common, but we were puzzled by their fierce hostility to the Soviet Union, while they were perturbed by our tolerant attitude towards Communism. They were even more perturbed by our friendship with Mirski, a schoolteacher, and Joseph, a mature student, who were typical of the Jewish Communists of our town. We knew that they were members of the banned Communist Party, but we considered them as selfless, if somewhat eccentric, visionaries, and the Garson brothers' hostility towards them seemed to us unreasonable.

Our views changed after Samuel told us his life story. A large part of it described how a Utopian dream of a better world turned into a nightmare. This had a frightening effect on us. Samuel, in contrast to his brother Mike, was never one to mince his words and he began his story by making the point that the Bolsheviks were a conspiratorial clique. They had replaced the liberal government of the provisional Prime Minister, Kerenski, by their brutal 'Dictatorship of the Proletariat', thus sabotaging Russia's progress towards democracy.

He then went on to describe the enormous suffering undergone by the Jewish population and he explained the part played by Jewish Bolsheviks, like Mirski and Joseph, in inflicting pain and misery on their brethren.

Among Samuel's pre-Revolutionary friends were some Jewish Bolsheviks. He was impressed by their idealism and dedication and got on well with them. It was only after the Bolsheviks gained power that he realised that they had undergone a profound transformation. A capacity for blind obedience and fanatical zeal had eliminated all sense of reason, logic and personal conscience. They viewed the Jewish national culture as their natural enemy and were determined to destroy it. They cruelly persecuted Jewish traders, religious leaders, Zionists and any individuals who could be classed as capitalist or bourgeois 'enemies of the people'. Because of their intimate knowledge of Jewish organisations, they were given the task of uprooting them. Leading members of these organisations were imprisoned. Some were shot.

The Garson brothers realised that it was too dangerous to

remain in the now-renamed Petrograd, and moved 200 miles north to the provincial town of Petrozavodsk. There they led a precarious existence and nearly died of starvation during the famine of 1920-1922.

The majority of the Jewish population, who had been rejoicing at the full emancipation granted by the Kerenski government, saw all hopes dashed by the Bolshevik takeover and by the subsequent attack on their traditions and culture. The fact that some of the persecutors were their own people added insult to injury. However, the biggest disaster for the Jewish community was the civil war.

For the warring factions, harmless and innocent Jews did not exist; they were all guilty by association. The Bolsheviks associated them with the Jewish bourgeois exploiters of the working classes; the Tsarist 'White Guards' identified them with the Jewish Bolsheviks. The Jewish civilian population paid a terrible price; more than 60,000 of them were murdered in a series of indiscriminate massacres, mostly in the Ukraine and in Russia.

In 1921 Lenin introduced his 'New Economic Policy' (NEP), a brave attempt to move to a free market system. Conditions began to improve and, taking advantage of the more relaxed atmosphere, the Garson brothers moved back to Leningrad (the former St Petersburg). The easier conditions did not last long. All the while, Stalin was consolidating his grip on power and in 1929 he abolished the NEP. To stifle all opposition, he unleashed his own more deadly version of the party's favourite twin weapons: propaganda and terror. For the Jews, one of the frightening features of Stalin's rule was his fierce antisemitism and his tendency to use Jewish Communists to do his dirty work.

As soon as he started the first show trials, the party organised mass demonstrations. The crowds, which spilled onto the streets, soon took on the character of a bloodthirsty mob. Egged on by Communist Party activists, they demanded death sentences for the accused and for all the enemies of the working classes.

Next, an epidemic of denunciations hit the country. The party created a siege mentality of uncertainty and fear by making wild allegations of enemy infiltration, spying, sabotage and corruption. Then they invited citizens to weed out the 'enemies of the people'. In no time, decent and friendly citizens were transformed into enthusiastic informers, rushing to denounce each other. Children, encouraged by their teachers, informed on their parents. The terror reached the remotest parts of the Soviet Union. Some of the accused were shot, but most of them were sentenced to hard labour and sent to work on Stalin's grandiose engineering projects.

Samuel and Mike worked on those projects in northern Russia and saw the convicts dying in their thousands of hunger, fatigue, cold and disease. All the time the wheels of terror were rolling on, providing an inexhaustible supply of slave labour. Before they left Russia, they witnessed the horrors of the mass killings and deportations of peasants during the forced collectivization of agriculture in the early 1930s. They realised that as ex-members of a 'capitalist' family, they were in danger and had better get out as soon as possible. Their application for an exit permit was granted and, despite some last minute snags, they managed to leave Russia. They considered Lithuania a dull provincial backwater without any demand for their expertise, and expected to be handicapped by their lack of the native language.

On arrival in Kaunas, the brothers were pleasantly surprised at the cohesion of the Jewish community and at the multicultural nature of the town. True, there were no grand engineering projects, but there was plenty of work to keep them busy, and thanks to the cross-fertilisation of the different cultures, everybody around them was bilingual or multilingual. Their knowledge of Russian, German and Yiddish enabled them to communicate without any difficulty.

Samuel's story created a deep impression, but people who live in peaceful and comfortable circumstances are not inclined to dwell too long on ugly and disturbing facts of life. Despite the threatening developments across our eastern and western borders, our attitude remained one of naïvety and of wishful thinking. Wiser counsels among us warned that we were sitting on the edge of a volcano which was liable to blow up suddenly, but their warnings were ignored. However, the story of Samuel did have positive results: we became suspicious of starry-eyed idealism and of ideological obsessions with Utopian visions, and our opinion of our Communist friends underwent a profound change.

Meanwhile, Mirski and Joseph felt that they had to prove their commitment to the Communist cause by going to Russia to help build the ideal society. They arrived in Moscow at the beginning of Stalin's 'great purge' and were arrested. We heard that Joseph was shot and that Mirski finished up in a Siberian Gulag (forced labour camp).

Portent of Danger

My education took a number of twists and turns. When I arrived back from France at the age of six, I spoke French only and was straight away enrolled into a German primary school. It was considered the best in town and the teaching staff were very helpful. Nevertheless, it took me quite a long time to settle in. Then came another upheaval. With the advent of the German Nazi movement, the Jewish children left to join Hebrew or Lithuanian schools. I joined the latter and had to have a crash course in Lithuanian (not such an easy language for a French-speaking child) in order to pass the entrance exams. At home I spoke Yiddish with my grandparents, Russian with my stepfather and French with my mother. Quite a mélange!

Once I got to grips with the Lithuanian language, I settled down nicely and found life at 'State School Number Three' quite agreeable. The lessons lasted from 8 a.m. to 1 p.m., six days a week. My pet hatred was reserved for homework. I reckoned that

I had better things to do, like playing with my friends, reading books, listening to my old and scratchy opera recordings or to the radio.

The facilities and educational standards at the state school were not as good as at the private school, but for a mainly peasant country determined to develop fast, it was important to set up a nationwide network of educational institutions, even if it meant sacrificing some quality in favour of quantity.

The respect for learning was widespread. It was felt not only by the authorities and teaching staff, but also by the pupils. There was hardly any truancy, vandalism, bullying or any other disruptive behaviour. The need for discipline was accepted as a matter of course and consequently the option of punishment was seldom exercised. For some reason our school was very popular with the minorities, especially the Polish and Jewish communities. They got on well together, as well as with the Lithuanian majority.

This sounds like a golden age of education but, regrettably, there were a lot of snags. The whole system was rigid and under such strict central control that there was little room for local initiative. The curriculum was geared to pupils of average ability; the bright boys and girls were not sufficiently stimulated and the slower pupils found it difficult to keep up. If they did not pass the year-end exams, they had to remain in the class for another year. The system penalised the underachievers and late developers. They were labelled as failures and their will to continue was undermined.

To my disappointment, the two foreign languages taught at our school were German and French. My request for English lessons was not even considered. So I decided I might as well do some of my homework during the language lessons. Our teacher of German was a young man just out of college and his knowledge of the language was not really up to scratch. We reached a tacit agreement: if I refrained from correcting his German, he would allow me freedom to engage in activities of my own choosing.

So far as French was concerned, there was no need for an agreement. The teacher was an old dear, an expert in French, but too aged and short-sighted to keep track of my classroom activities.

Any remaining homework I usually managed to do during the two or three weekly Religious Education lessons. The non-Catholics in our class, e.g. the Jews, the Russian Orthodox and the two atheists, were excused and kept me company.

It was an open secret that the term 'atheist' was a euphemism for members of the banned Communist Party. Their number in our class was small – never more than three – but they impressed us with their sense of purpose, their dedication to their ideology and the courage of their convictions. Despite invitations to join them, I had no intention of obliging; my attitude had been conditioned by Samuel Garson's hostility to Communism and his dislike of all ideologies. He maintained that their claim to the exclusive knowledge of truth encouraged intolerance and bigotry.

The uncompromising views of the Communists were in stark contrast to the generally relaxed school atmosphere, which was probably due to the fact that quite a lot of our teachers were members of various opposition parties, and their liberal outlook seemed to prevail. Our teacher of the Lithuanian language was a prominent member of the Social Democratic Party. When his political activities became restricted as a consequence of the right-wing military coup, he found an outlet for his cosmopolitan views by introducing the international language of Esperanto to the country, and by promoting the Boy Scout movement.

This enthusiasm for Esperanto was not shared by his pupils, but they joined the Boy Scouts – and so did I. The movement flourished, but unfortunately it was not immune from the attentions of the National Party activists. As their influence increased, our Scoutmaster resigned. I left and joined the Young Zionist movement, only to find myself in the middle of an acrimonious split between the right and left wings of the organisation. The fierce animosity which followed the split perturbed me and I decided to leave.

Out of school, I had plenty of activities to keep me busy.

I caught the reading bug at the age of eight and never managed to get rid of it. Fortunately, about half a mile from us there was a large, private library specialising in German books. I indiscriminately devoured book after book, cheap pulp fiction, classical novels and plays, modern works, etc.

Some years later, in my teens, I caught the music bug. The opera house in Kaunas seemed to me the pinnacle of romance and glamour. It was difficult to obtain tickets and mother and I used to take turns to queue at the box office, especially if there were concerts by foreign celebrities. When we got our first radio, it seemed to me a miracle. I could not get over the fact that within our own home, we now had access to a new and exciting world of music and speech.

On graduating from the grammar school, I enrolled in the Architectural Department of the University of Kaunas and adapted well to the new demands of student existence. At the same time I became anxious about the pace and scope of ominous developments. Anti-Jewish agitation was reaching a degree of unprecedented viciousness. Nazi-inspired racial antisemitism was spreading like a contagious disease across the German border and adding to the traditional religious and economic anti-semitism.

The autumn of 1939 saw the fall and partition of Poland, which left Lithuania dangerously exposed. Traumatised Polish Jews who managed to flee to Lithuania from the German-occupied region of Poland were bringing tales of Nazi atrocities. To add to our worries, Mr Wallner, a Volksdeutscher (ethnic German) friend of the family, informed us that orders had arrived from Berlin instructing the German community to leave Lithuania and rejoin the Vaterland. He also disclosed that at a meeting they had decided to obey the order.

We were stunned by Wallner's information. The ethnic Germans were Lithuanian citizens and had lived and prospered in the country for centuries. There had been a cultural affinity between them and the secular Jews from the time when the ideas of the German Enlightenment were adopted by the Haskalah movement. Some common shared traits like competence, reliability and a passion for education also served to strengthen the relationship, and accounted for the fact that Jewish enterprises discriminated in favour of German workers and vice-versa. It was only in the late 1930s that the adverse effect of Nazi propaganda resulted in some deterioration in the relationship.

There was one positive development to lighten the gloom. While Germany and the Soviet Union were annexing chunks of Polish territory, Stalin decided to restore to Lithuania its ancient capital, Vilnius. Despite severe misgivings about Stalin's true intentions, it was a momentous event, not only for the Lithuanians but also for the Jews. The iron curtain between the Vilnius (Vilna) Jews and the ones from independent Lithuania was lifted and after a complete separation of 19 years, the Litvaks could again resume contact.

As for my time as a student, I soon discovered that even at university it was impossible to escape from antisemitic agitation. The academic atmosphere was being poisoned by a vociferous gang of Nazi sympathisers, who had embarked on a concerted campaign of harassment and intimidation of the Jewish students.

I was worried by these unpleasant developments, but I failed to recognise the implications for the future. My complacency was probably due to my naïve trust in human nature, and also to two facts which conditioned my thinking: I had not experienced any antisemitism at school, and no pogroms had been perpetrated on Lithuanian soil.

The liberally-minded, non-Jewish students were just as complacent. They could not believe that the crude, irrational hate propaganda could flourish for any length of time in the highest, most prestigious learning establishment of the land, and thought that it would wither away for lack of support. Their view was never put to the test. The Red Army marched in and everything came to an abrupt end.

CHAPTER TWO

HOME-GROWN
BRUTALITY

NAZI OCCUPATION AND
LOCAL COLLABORATION

The War

The Soviet occupation in June 1940 was a devastating blow. The dead hand of total Communist control turned the country into an economic and cultural wasteland. Nearly every aspect of our lives was turned upside down. The larger properties and private enterprises were confiscated without compensation; independent newspapers and organisations were banned, and religious activities restricted.

Some Jews, believing that the Soviet regime would abolish racial discrimination, welcomed the arrival of the Red Army. Of course, the Nazi sympathisers went into hiding or kept their heads down, but this was of little comfort to the majority of the Jews. By virtue of their position as traders, shopkeepers, entrepreneurs and property owners, they were persecuted as much, if not more, than any other section of the population.

Quite a lot of the housing stock in central Kaunas had been owned by Jews, and when the janitors and caretakers were appointed property managers, they acquired the power to evict the original owners from their dwellings – and did so quite often. In that respect the Garsons were lucky. They were allowed to remain in their flat, but they knew that their days of freedom were numbered, not only because they had been the owners of two large apartment blocks, but also because of the reputations of Samuel and Mike as anti-Soviet agitators.

Meanwhile we got a taste of life under a regime based on terror. The borders were sealed, the secret police (KGB) arrived to weed out the 'enemies of the people'. Relentless Communist propaganda was assailing our senses via the press, the radio, the cinema and powerful loudspeakers erected in public places. The personality cult of Stalin, 'the genius of mankind', was in full swing. There was no escaping the endless statistics of record-breaking production, and the contrasting of enslaved and starving masses in capitalist countries with the happy and free life in the workers' paradise.

Some of my friends with impeccable bourgeois credentials were beginning to eulogise the Communist ideology. I was dumbfounded by this sudden change and wondered whether it was brought about by the power of indoctrination, a mixture of fear and expediency, or genuine conviction. A frank conversation would have given me some idea, but in the prevailing climate of fear. this would have been dangerous.

In the middle of June 1941, exactly a year after the Red Army marched into Lithuania, the purges of the 'enemies of the people' started. The secret police arrested about 30,000 people and deported them to Russian and Siberian forced labour camps. Among them were Lithuanian and Jewish 'capitalists', religious leaders of all denominations, leading intellectuals, Jewish Zionists and members of the Lithuanian National Party. We knew that our turn would come sooner or later, and we lived in fear of the midnight knock of the KGB. Meanwhile the propaganda effort was becoming more and more incongruous. It went into overdrive to try to prove to us how fortunate we were to live safe and secure in a workers' paradise. At the height of the purges, a special place was reserved on the public address system for the 'Motherland' song. I'll never forget the words – "I know no other country where men can breathe more freely." The members of my family were not deported, but the event which saved us from a Siberian slave labour camp was even more deadly.

In the early hours of Sunday 22 June 1941, a number of explsions shook our house and woke everybody. Black smoke was drifting from the direction of the military airport. We realised that it was under attack. Full of foreboding, the five of us – grandfather, grandmother, mother, my stepfather and I – decided to walk over to the rest of the Garson family for a consultation. It was about ten minutes from our home, but we met a lot of people carrying suitcases and heading east.

The arguments started as soon as we arrived at our destination. Our hopes that the war would bypass us were in vain. From the radio broadcasts it soon became clear that the German army was advancing, the Russians were retreating. Should we try to escape, leaving all our possessions behind? After a long argument it was decided that we should stay. The only dissenting voice was that of my stepfather. Despite his hatred of Communism, he argued that the Nazis were a bigger menace than the Russians, and that he would rather take his chances with the class murderers under Stalin's control than with the race murderers under Hitler's command. He was overruled by the older members of the Garson family who had lived through the German occupation during World War One. They maintained that German culture and civilisation were too old and stable to be wiped out in eight years by Hitler. There would be a lot of danger and deprivation, but it would be possible to survive.

We dispersed, feeling slightly reassured by the decision.

Of the 14 members of the Garson and Strom families gathered that morning of 22 June 1941, I was the only one to survive the war.

The Start of the Terror

Our difficulties started at once, but they came from an unexpected direction. The Russians pulled out of Lithuania without a fight. Kaunas suffered no destruction and no damage. The German army moved through quickly, to carry the war deep into Russia. The population of Lithuania welcomed the arrival of the German army with great enthusiasm. For them it meant liberation from one year of Soviet terror; for the Jewish community, it proved to be a step on the road towards Hitler's 'Final Solution of the Jewish question'.

To our surprise, when our troubles began, they came from a volunteer force of well-organised, armed and uniformed Lithuanians, who appeared from nowhere and started a campaign of terror against the Jews, blaming them for misdeeds committed by the Communist regime. We lived in a narrow, quiet side street and were sheltered from the horror around us. We heard rumours of pogroms, stories of atrocities, but we could not believe them. We thought that they were lies, exaggerations or isolated incidents.

During the night of 25 June, Lithuanian thugs broke into the Jewish quarter of Viljampole, a suburb of Kaunas – Slabodke in Yiddish – and massacred about 1,000 people: men, women and children. The irony of this tragedy is that these first victims of the pogroms were the most implacable enemies of the Communists – the rabbinical students, their teachers and families.

The next day, about 60 Jews were herded into a garage courtyard for forced labour. With blows raining down on them and a jeering crowd watching, they had to clean up the horse manure covering the forecourt. When the work was finished, the militia started a new bout of beatings, using crowbars, spades and rifles. Many were killed on the spot. The survivors and wounded were taken to Fort V and shot. Around the city of Kaunas, a number of large fortifications had been built to defend the town in Tsarist times. During the Nazi occupation, these forts were used as places of horrendous brutality and mass murder. Among the victims that day was my mother's older brother, George Strom.

In the provinces, the atrocities were even worse. In some places, whole Jewish communities were wiped out, their possessions looted and their homes occupied. In Kaunas, over 2,000 Jews were killed in the first week alone. Many thousands more were arrested and their property looted. They were taken to various forts in the surroundings of the town and then shot.

That week I decided to visit my Aunt Sonia, my mother's younger sister, who was in hospital recovering from an operation. The centre of town was full of armed Lithuanian militia. I was arrested near the entrance to the hospital and taken to a police station. I became alarmed when four terrified Jews, two men and two women, were dragged in by armed partisans. They knew all about the killings and explained to me the danger of our situation. We all calmed down, however, when a middle-aged policeman who took over the guard duties assured us that he would take us to clean out some army barracks, then take us safely home. He got us some food for lunch and took us home in the evening. Auntie Sonia was not so lucky; she was killed shortly after. Nor were the other Jews arrested that day. They were taken to Fort VI and shot.

The story of the torture and death of another group, estimated at 1,500, was told down to the smallest detail by 70 eyewitnesses who were among the arrested Jews. They were later released because, during the 1918 War of Independence, they had volunteered to join the Lithuanian army. The 1,500 were taken to Fort VII, squeezed into a hollow within the compound and kept there for days in the open, without food or water, surrounded by heavily-armed Lithuanian militia who shot anybody who moved or talked. There were many dead and wounded, the latter begging the guards to put them out of their misery.

Just before the mass execution started, the 70 Jews who

managed to prove that they had fought in the War of Independence were released, more dead than alive, from the effects of thirst, hunger and terror. This time there was no room for doubt. However unbelievable the story sounded, we could not dismiss it; the witnesses were people of integrity and judgement.

News of other arrests and shootings continued to reach us. The list of missing relatives and friends grew every day. The continuous toll of disasters outstripped our capacity to react to them. Unable to comprehend these events, we became confused and very frightened. In desperation, the leaders of the Jewish community appealed to the Bishop of Kaunas for help. His reply that it was "Not in his power to intervene against a spontaneous expression of people's wrath", deepened our anxiety.

The Nazis in charge of us, the SS and Gestapo, belonged to the specially indoctrinated and trained executive arm of the party, feared not only outside but also inside Germany. Their privileged position behind the front line depended on their willingness to terrorise the population.

It seemed the Nazis looked on with amazement at the unexpected zeal of the murderous Lithuanian militia. This was a considerable bonus and it made their plans to confine us to a ghetto a lot easier. The plan could now be presented as a goodwill gesture to protect us from the militia or 'partisans' as they liked to call themselves.

The origin of this partisan movement dated back to the days of the Soviet occupation, when an underground resistance network was set up to fight the hated Communist invaders. This movement was controlled by the Lithuanian Activist Front (LAF), a far-right organisation, which worked hand in hand with the Nazis and may even have had prior knowledge of German war plans.

On Sunday 22 June 1941, on the first day of hostilities, partisans were already in evidence. They were armed and wore the khaki-coloured uniform of the Lithuanian army. They quickly occupied the radio stations and claimed to have liberated their country from the Jewish-Bolshevik usurpers, whose time had come to be punished. There were not many leading Bolsheviks around, as they had managed to flee. The Jews, however, were a handy scapegoat, who for years had been blamed for every vice in the land. The partisans had in their power a defenceless and easily identifiable minority, wealthy enough to make the pogroms very lucrative.

The accusation that the Jews were Bolsheviks and had betrayed Lithuania was contradicted by the fact that proportionately more Jews than Lithuanians were deported to Siberia. However, Jews had been prominent in the tiny, illegal pre-war Communist Party of Lithuania and some rose to high office during Soviet rule, but they were no better or worse than the Lithuanian Communists. Both executed orders from Moscow and inflicted pain and suffering without fear or favour on all sections of the population.

The Ghetto Deadline

Once the initial frenzied phase was over, things moved fast. Now that the Nazis had us fully under their control, they were able to enforce further regulations to humiliate and dictate to us. In July 1941 the Germans issued the following edicts:

*All Jews to wear the yellow Star of David

*All Jews will be moved into a ghetto in Viljampole (Slobodka)

*Jews are prohibited from:

    (a) using public places

    (b) using public transport

    (c) walking on pavements

    (d) selling property

    (e) owning radios

The official announcement about the establishment of the ghetto was made by Lithuanian officials on 10 July. Shortly afterwards, senior members of the Gestapo summoned a Jewish delegation and, after quoting Lithuanian accusations about Jewish-Bolshevik responsibility in persecuting the population during Soviet rule, they made the point that the Jews would be safer in the ghetto, where they would be protected from the wrath of the Lithuanians. The deadline was fixed for 15 August. Any Jew found outside the ghetto after that date would be shot. Meanwhile the excesses against the Jews would be stopped. The Jews were told to select their own council, through which all future orders and edicts would be issued.

The Nazis' promises sounded reassuring and the creation of a ghetto seemed the lesser of two evils. At the same time, we were so disorientated and frightened by the deadly excesses of the partisans that the prospect of being locked up behind barbed wire, and even the loss of our property and belongings, seemed preferable to exposure to the Lithuanian militia.

The July edicts were followed by more restrictions. The tactics of the Nazis, designed to demoralise and dehumanise us by tightening the screw notch by notch, were in full swing. One of the edicts, the prohibition to shop in the market, resulted in tragedy for 26 Jews. Driven by hunger, they had tried to buy some food from a nearby farm. They were arrested, taken to Fort IX and shot.

The deadline of 15 August was approaching and over 30,000 Jews had to leave their homes to move into an area which had previously housed a population of about 10,000. We had to share a small wooden house with three families. It meant leaving most of our belongings behind. The removal lasted a few days. The streets were full of horse-drawn carriages loaded to the brim, rolling towards the ghetto, followed by harassed Jews carrying heavy bundles.

On 15 August 1941, the barbed wire was completed, the guards in position, and the gate shut. We were trapped, imprisoned, at the mercy of the Gestapo henchmen. But at the time we were too occupied with coping with the atrocious conditions, the chaos, overcrowding and hunger. We were too busy trying to survive to worry about the loss of our homes and belongings. What worried us very much was our prospects for the future.

We wanted to believe the German promises, but after the experiences of past events, we had become very nervous and full of suspicion. We realised that our life in the ghetto would be much more difficult and dangerous than we had imagined, but most of us still believed that the Nazis' need for our labour would ensure our survival. Little did we know that our fate was to be decided by fanatical Nazi bureaucrats who had managed to brain-wash a whole generation of Germans and turn them into willing accomplices.

The First 'Actions'

On 18 August, three days after the closing in of the ghetto, the SS and partisans arrived to pick up 500 Jews for a specially demanding job: to sort out the records and files of the town hall. The Jewish council was told that the men must be well educated; the work would be indoors, and three meals would be provided. My classmate David and I decided to join the group, but I arrived late and was No 539 in the line. Only 534 men were taken, including David. They were not seen again. We assumed that they had been taken for forced labour. Some time later, Lithuanian witnesses informed us of their fate. They were taken to Fort IV and shot.

The day after the '500 action' – also called the 'Intellectuals Action' – the German police and a large number of partisans descended on the ghetto and proceeded to search every house for gold, silver and jewellery; even wedding rings were taken. The searches lasted two weeks and became progressively more vicious. There were arrests, beatings and shootings. After the first search, as we were trying to tidy up, two Lithuanian partisans walked unexpectedly into our house and arrested me. In her panic, my mother took out an expensive Omega watch, which she had carefully hidden, and ran after the two men. To our surprise, they pocketed the watch and let me go. My mother's quick action saved me from a one-way trip to Fort IX.

After the searches were over, the administrator of the ghetto, Obersturmführer (Lieutenant) Jordan, declared that he was not satisfied with the results. A more serious search would begin, and for every valuable found, 100 Jews would be shot. Before carrying out this threat, he would wait for two days to allow the Jewish council to organise a final collection and hand it in. We knew that he meant it, and handed in the few hidden items. The Germans collected them, then came back for the final search. They finally left on 5 September.

Conditions in the overcrowded ghetto were rapidly deteriorating. We were locked inside a large prison and expected to survive on starvation rations which, whether by accident or design, didn't always reach us. Just as the lack of food became critical, the Nazis unwittingly provided us with a lifeline. The Jewish council was ordered to register men between the ages of 14 and 60 and women between the ages of 15 and 55 for forced labour in town and at the airport.

There were some privileged minorities who did not have to share the hardship of the majority. They were the Jewish council and the bureaucracy administering the affairs of the ghetto and dealing with Nazi edicts and orders, and the Jewish police enforcing those orders on their brethren. They were entitled to extra rations and were exempted from forced labour. Another privileged group consisted of the kapos (leaders) appointed to take charge of work brigades and of workers selected for the cleaner and easier jobs in town. These privileged people looked more healthy, well-fed and well-dressed. The contrast between them and the emaciated and dirty airport workers was striking.

The Airport Brigade

The majority of the ghetto workforce was assigned to the airport, to difficult, back-breaking shift work, going on day and night, under relentless supervision. My job was to cut and chop wood for the winter stockpile. It was hard work, but I could occasionally smuggle some firewood into the ghetto. Due to tight security, the airport was inaccessible to civilians, so if any of our workers wanted to contact Lithuanian friends, they had to make their exit while on the way to work. The fact that we were guarded by a detachment of trigger-happy partisans made this an extremely risky undertaking.

One bright autumn morning as we were marching towards the airport, I noticed, a few rows in front of me, a short, stocky young man taking off his yellow Star of David. He was conspicuous because of his ruddy complexion and his smart two-piece suit, totally unsuitable for the dirty airport work. As we were going round a tight corner, he stepped on the pavement and disappeared into a side street. Expecting trouble, we quickly closed ranks, but a look at the guards calmed our fears. "I know this fellow; it's Joseph Kagan," remarked my neighbour. "He's crazy; the way he's carrying on, he won't last long." A worker who had helped Joseph to remove his yellow patches overheard us and joined in: "I know him better than you; he might have a second-class temperament, but he's got a first-class brain and that will see him through." And indeed Joseph Kagan survived the imprisonment, made his way to England and became Lord Kagan of Elland.

The Jewish kapo of all kapos at the airport, a man called Bergmann, was in charge of 4,000 to 4,500 people. His was a position of immense privilege and power, but also of danger, since he was the direct link between the German bosses and the workers. He had under him a team of 40 kapos, and was allowed to move around without guards.

My next job was night work, digging trenches for the airport drains. On the very first night, I was working in a ditch about a couple of hundred yards from a gang of Russian prisoners of war. There were thousands of them working at the huge airport. There was no shelter for them. Day and night they were kept in the open, in barbed wire enclosures.

The Hitler Youth

There were about two dozen prisoners of war levelling the soil not far from my trench. They were guarded by members of the Hitler Youth, teenagers in brown Nazi uniforms, who were buzzing around, kicking and beating the prisoners. It was no use. The emaciated figures were unable to dig the hard ground.

A whistle blew for a meal break. The POWs formed a line for a drink of watery soup. The first to be served staggered, the soup can dropped to the ground, spilling a few drops on the boots of a Hitler Youth. The teenager picked up a spade and buried it in the skull of the prostrate Russian. About half a dozen prisoners threw themselves on the ground to grab the soup can. This triggered off an orgy of killing. Half the guards took up spades and set upon the unfortunate POWs, aiming at their heads and necks; and the other guards started beating the prisoners with their rifle butts. The supervisors and officers seemed unconcerned; they just looked on and did nothing.

Overcome with fright and revulsion, I turned away to continue digging my trench. It was not only the moral degradation of the torturers which shocked me, it was also the moral and physical collapse of the victims. I could not understand why young, trained soldiers who had nothing to lose did not turn against their tormentors. It was only later, when I was in a similar situation, that I became aware of the devastating effect of hunger and depravation on the victim.

My second encounter with the Hitler Youth took place about

a month later – a month which had weakened us quite a lot. Lack of food, the cold wet autumn and the hard work in the open were claiming their toll. Every one of us was depressed by the thought of the approaching winter and by the events in the ghetto. There was no respite from the terror tactics of the Gestapo: edicts, searches, actions, arrests and shootings.

I was digging a trench as usual when I noticed that our Lithuanian guard was being replaced by the brown-uniformed Hitler Youth. This was our first contact with the most indoctrinated section of the Nazis. Since childhood they had been corrupted by the theory of the German master race, destined to rule the world, and by the concept of the inferior, subhuman races like the Jews, the Gypsies and the Slavs.

To our surprise, they were well behaved and did not bother us. One of them, a youth of about 16 or 17, jumped into my trench and demanded to see my leather gloves. Amazed, but also frightened, I tried to put him off by pointing out the torn seams and the worn lining. My attitude changed when he said, "I want your gloves because of the brown leather which matches the colour of my uniform. I'll give you my knitted grey gloves and bring you some sandwiches in the afternoon."

The exchange took place, and he walked off. At midday, when the guards changed, I lost all hope of ever seeing him again. Then, as it was getting dark, he appeared, handed me a bag of cheese sandwiches and quickly vanished.

Liquidation of the Small Ghetto

In the middle of September 1941, Obersturmführer Jordan supplied the Jewish council with 5,000 work passes, with instructions to distribute them to key personnel. The passes, certifying that the bearer was usefully employed, were referred to as 'lifesavers'. By the time the council bureaucracy, the kapos and key persons got their share, there were none left for the manual airport workers. I did not get a pass, and it made the prospect of having to face a winter at the airport even worse. It soon became clear why the passes were called 'lifesavers'.

On 26 September, the German police and Lithuanian militia entered the ghetto and arrested a large number of Jews. All the holders of the Jordan work certificates were released. Some 1,000 Jews without passes were taken to Fort IX and shot.

Even worse was to come eight days later. On 4 October, as we were returning from the airport, we saw a column of black smoke over the ghetto. When we got inside, we discovered that the Nazis were in the process of liquidating the small ghetto, a separate enclave linked to the main ghetto by a wooden bridge built over a main road. The wooden hospital building in the enclave was on fire, with the doctors, nurses and patients trapped inside, behind nailed-up doors and windows.

On that day the ghetto lost 1,500 people. But, as on 26 September, only Jews without Jordan passes were taken. Anybody who could produce one was released and allowed to cross the bridge to the main ghetto. The whole 'action' took place in front of our eyes. Every one of us had friends and relatives amongst the people burned alive and amongst the other victims of the action. We could only watch with impotent rage as the Jews of the small ghetto were taken under heavy guard to their death at Fort IX. Next morning the police had to use force to round up the dazed and sullen workers for the morning shift at the airport.

Towards the end of October, Uncle Mike and my stepfather brought me some good news. They had managed to get employment at the Heeresbau, the engineering, construction and maintenance section of the German army. The Heeresbau intended to expand their workforce by using skilled Jewish labour for their major projects – repairs to property, maintenance of public buildings, conversions of schools into hospitals etc.

That was the end of my misery at the airport. I received a

Jordan pass and joined a group of civil engineers and architects whose task it was to measure the many abandoned army barracks around Kaunas, prepare drawings and plans, and report on the condition of the buildings. My job was to draw the barracks floor by floor and provide accurate measurements.

CHAPTER THREE

REIGN OF TERROR

THE KAUNAS GHETTO

The Big 'Action'

Just as I was beginning my job with the Heeresbau, the Nazis started preparing one of the most terrible 'actions'. On 27 October 1941, the Jewish council issued posters announcing a census of the whole ghetto population which was to take place at 6.00 a.m. on 28 October. Everybody, even the sick and the infants, had to line up in workplace formation on Democracy Square. All house doors had to be left open to allow inspection; anybody found inside after 6.00 a.m. would be shot on the spot.

We were up most of the night. Our main worry was my grandparents, as they were frail and walked with difficulty. We had no hiding place in the house, so we had to take them with us and support them as best we could. Early that morning about 27,000 people gathered in the square, lined up according to their workplace.

The German police and a large contingent of Lithuanian militia arrived. The SS man in charge, Hauptscharführer (Master Sergeant) Rauca, ordered the columns to march past him and started directing the people to the right or the left. Jordan was standing nearby, helping him. There was no obvious reason for this division, but nevertheless there was tension in the air, a feeling of impending disaster.

A commotion broke out when Rauca started separating members of the same family. Despite the dense cordon, the separated members of the same family tried to join up again. The guards would not allow it and forced them back, savagely beating everybody around them. Men, women and children, their faces covered in blood, were crying and pleading to be reunited. We realised that this was no census and formed the impression that children, women and elderly people predominated on the left side.

It was nearly dark when our turn came. We were hungry, numb with cold, shocked and frightened by the violence around us. Rauca looked at us and indicated to the right, but as we were turning, he suddenly picked out uncle Max Garson (an older brother of my stepfather), his wife and two sisters, four middle-aged but fit-looking people, and directed them to the left. Max started pleading and pulled out his Jordan pass. It was no use. I was already on the right side, but I jumped through the cordon and ran towards them, shouting that they were my parents. I managed to reach the left side and grab Max by the arm, but the line of guards was closing behind us and we were all trapped on the left. Then one of the guards set upon me with his rifle butt, shouting that I was meant to go to the right and should not be on the left side. He forced me back to the right.

I shall never know how he remembered me, whether he was following me, or why he bothered to chase me back, but his action saved my life. I joined my family, dazed and bruised, but all I could think about was the terrible last look in Uncle Max's eyes when I had to let go of his arm. A look of despair, but also of surrender, of hopeless resignation. Mentally and physically exhausted, shocked and confused, we went home, trying to convince ourselves that the 'selection' had been too random, that too many able-bodied men went to the left and too many old people to the right to draw any final conclusions. The people on the left side were taken under heavy guard to the empty, small ghetto. In the morning, to our dismay, the long column started out in the direction of Fort IX.

The details of the massacre of the 10,000 Jews soon leaked out. A teenager who managed to escape saw it from his hiding place. When he reached the ghetto, the horrified Jewish council asked him to keep his experiences secret. But it was impossible to hide it for long.

The Germans were so sure of their eventual victory that they did not worry too much about secrecy. Democracy Square was visible from outside the ghetto, and the 'Big Action' had been witnessed by many Lithuanians. The road to Fort IX was a public highway; the fort was not far from an inhabited area, and some Lithuanians could see what was going on within the enclosure. Within days the gruesome details were available to the ghetto inhabitants. Some chose not to believe the witnesses' accounts and clung on to the hope that the 10,000 had been taken for forced labour.

The mood in the ghetto was one of apathy and depression, but also of defiance. Hardly anybody bothered to turn up for work. As we were wandering around looking for our relatives and friends, the extent of our loss began to emerge. Our immediate family was badly hit, especially on the Strom side. We lost many aunts, uncles and cousins, as well as close friends and acquaintances. Especially depressing was the loss of my youngest cousin, Liova, and his widowed mother. He was a charming little boy about ten years my junior and I used to spend a large part of the summer holidays playing with him and taking him for rides on my bicycle.

As for the fourteen members of our family who took the decision to remain in Kaunas and try to survive under Nazi rule, only seven were still alive. At a stroke, we lost half of our immediate family. Our trauma was compounded by the fact that our killers were our Lithuanian neighbours, ordinary young men who had volunteered to join the Nazis. (It was Nazi policy to turn citizens of occupied countries into accomplices. Although the supervision was German, up to 80 per cent of the killing machine was kept going by non-Germans – Latvians, Lithuanians, Ukrainians, Croats, Hungarians, Rumanians etc.)

For my family and for me, the 'Big Action' was the defining event. It would have been of some comfort if I could have identified our killers as sadists, psychopaths or misfits, but I couldn't. The fact that ordinary, normal people could be turned into killers of an innocent, defenceless civilian population shattered my belief in 'benevolent and progressive' humanity. It seemed that the line between good and evil was a lot thinner than I had imagined, and that it was all too easy to indoctrinate ordinary people to cross that line into evil.

Final proof about the fate of the victims came from the Jewish brigade employed by Gestapo Headquarters in Kaunas on various menial jobs. In November they received a pile of clothing for sorting. They became suspicious when they noticed the local origin of the garments. On closer examination, they discovered that they had been given the clothing of the victims of the 'Big Action'. So, despite the efforts of the Jewish council to preserve secrecy, the whole ghetto discovered the truth. The trauma caused by this 'action' was even more severe than the one caused by the Lithuanian gangs in the summer, when they turned on their Jewish neighbours and massacred them in their thousands.

A colleague from the Heeresbau, a German Jew who had served as an officer in the Imperial German army, had only one piece of advice, "We must stop driving ourselves crazy trying to fathom out, trying to comprehend the events around us. It will be easier to bear the blows if we just accept that our world has gone mad."

The Nazis in charge became alarmed by the defiant attitude in the ghetto. They had a safe and pleasant time in Kaunas and dreaded a transfer to the front. Jordan and Rauca produced assurances that no more 'actions' would take place, but work had to be resumed.

This promise had only a limited effect. The deciding factor, forcing us to go to work, was the need to survive. The temperature started to fall, there was no food, no fuel in the ghetto. The only way to acquire the means of survival was to obtain them in town and smuggle them in. We resumed our work routine, but the gaps in the work brigades were a constant grim reminder that we had lost nearly half of our ghetto population. Of the 30,000 Jews imprisoned in the ghetto on 15 August 1941, only 16,500 were left alive.

On the Brink of Annihilation

On 18 August, we had suffered the 'Intellectuals Action'; 26 September, the '1,000 action'; and on 4 October, the liquidation of the small ghetto. The feelings of bewilderment and incomprehension generated by the first three 'actions' of the year 1941 were so overwhelming that we could not understand or believe the events taking place around us. It was after the trauma following the fourth 'action', the so-called 'Big Action' on 28 October 1941 that the true nature of our predicament began to be clearer. We had to face the fact that Nazi promises were worthless, that our 'civilised and cultured German protectors' had replaced the wanton terror of the partisans with a systematic programme of extermination.

Even at that stage there were some Jews who could not face reality and continued to indulge in wishful thinking. So far as our own family was concerned, there was a belief that we were facing unbridled evil and our reaction was total despair. Our nice little world, reconstructed from the ashes of World War One, had vanished, drowned in blood. The spectre of the complete corruptibility of man had replaced our belief in benevolent humanity. We were locked into a never-ending nightmare;

awake or asleep, we were haunted by the paralysing fear of death.

Grandpa, the most optimistic and cheerful of men, was badly affected by the general despondency. It was not unusual for me to see the members of our family upset or depressed, but Grandpa had always been an exception. Not only had he kept his cheerful manner in trying circumstances, but he had also been ready to advise and console those around him. It was most upsetting to see him so miserable and to see my mother bravely trying to fulfil his role as the comforter of the family.

Not everybody was as badly affected as we were. Some people in the community managed to find a measure of reassurance in their beliefs. A good example of this was provided by the religious Jews and by the Communists. As described earlier, the Lithuanian Jews were not noted for their religious zeal, but rather for their learning and the wisdom of their rabbinical scholars. The sages were now under great pressure to come up with an explanation for the calamities which befell the community, and to advise the Jewish council on how to cope with Nazi tactics. Despite studying the holy texts day and night, they failed to do so. All they could advise was that we should continue praying and hope that it may produce divine intervention.

Some Orthodox Jews found it difficult to reconcile the biblical concept of an omnipotent, omniscient God of justice and mercy with the indiscriminate slaughter of the Jewish people, and they became disaffected. The majority, however, managed to retain belief in their faith; for them the religious worship provided much needed solace and comfort.

The Lithuanian Communist party was small in numbers, but the members were highly motivated, dedicated and disciplined. These were all--important attributes for a movement which had been illegal during most of the existence of independent Lithuania and had to operate underground. Blessed with a simple vision of life, they had an equally simple solution to the problems of humanity. They maintained that by following faithfully the path of Marxism and Leninism, as the Soviet Union had done, the Utopian dreams of mankind would become reality.

Despite their small numbers and the loss of their leadership, who had fled with the Red Army, the ghetto Communists were less demoralised than the rest of us. They did not look upon the war as a disaster; on the contrary, according to their view of history, it was the inevitable, decisive encounter in the victorious march of Communism. When, a year later, a ghetto underground movement was launched, their skill and mastery of covert activities proved invaluable.

There were other internal factors which added to our stresses and tensions – the overcrowding, the cold, the hunger and mistrust between the Jewish functionaries and rank and file. The build-up of tension could have caused an internal explosion, but although there was a decline in moral standards and an increase in aggressive behaviour, it was thanks to the general restraint of the ghetto population that crime and violence were of a localised, containable nature.

The Jewish functionaries were a mixed lot of people – some good, some bad, some indifferent. But even the best of them, the ones selected for their honesty, integrity and competence, had not much chance of resisting the Nazis' terror methods and were sooner or later browbeaten into compliance.

Regrettably, there were a lot of self-seeking, unscrupulous individuals who in normal, peaceful conditions were nobodies, and for whom any opportunity of acquiring power was irresistible. They rushed in where decent people feared to tread and managed to secure important positions of power in the Jewish council, the police and work brigades. They surrounded themselves with like-minded cronies and began to dominate council policies and behaviour. Our reaction was to ridicule their display of vanity and pretensions. Our criticism and scorn, however strongly voiced, was in vain. Nothing, not even the fact that we were facing oblivion, could deflate their egos or change their attitudes.

The most serious internal disturbances happened during the distribution of the Jordan passes, when the blatant favouritism of the Jewish council became all too obvious to the whole ghetto population. The mistrust and tension between the Jews in power and the general population dated back to the creation of the council, when protectionism, favouritism and other negative features started to predominate.

At the beginning, it meant better housing, better jobs, better access to food and fuel for the relations and friends of the ruling clique, but once the bloody 'actions' and deportations started, it took on a more sinister implication. A good example was the 'Riga Action'. The lists of victims were prepared by the Jewish council and used by the Jewish police to round up the people. The ghetto population considered this as cooperation and even collaboration with the enemy, and it was bitterly resented. The issue of orders and edicts on behalf of the Nazis was also condemned on similar grounds. After the start of the mass killings, the criticisms became most severe, demanding a stop to all cooperation with the Germans. The most severe critic was a prominent lawyer called Golden. He claimed that cooperation with the worst Jew-killers in history could never be justified, and he accused the council members of betraying their fellow Jews.

The criticisms were rejected by the council. The issue of Nazi orders continued; the compiling of lists and rounding up for deportation also continued. The leaders of the council defended themselves by pointing out that somebody had to provide arbitration and guidance, and by insisting that direct Nazi rule would have been a lot worse. They maintained that they were appointed by the Jews in their hour of peril, and that they served as a buffer between the Nazis and the ghetto.

Winter of 'Calm'

During the winter of 1941-42, rumours were circulating that on the question of extermination or exploitation of the Jews, the Nazis had decided in favour of exploitation. We suspected that the rumours were spread by the Germans and ghetto leadership, to allay the shock of the 'Big Action' of 28 October 1941 and to make the workforce more amenable. Indeed, the period from November 1941 to October 1943 was free of mass executions and was called the 'calm period'. However, the systematic process of trying to degrade, humiliate and dehumanise the ghetto population continued as before. Jews were still arrested, beaten and killed, and on two occasions, in February and October 1942, a total of 870 people were rounded up and deported to Riga for slave labour.

In November 1941 we witnessed some events which again shocked us deeply. Jewish transports from France, Germany and Austria started arriving at Kaunas. They were led in long columns past the ghetto to Fort IX. Despite the long train journey, these people looked well-fed and dressed. Some of the ghetto Jews who managed to exchange a few words with them tried in vain to warn them. They had complete faith in the promises that they would be resettled near Kaunas, and continued the march in a confident mood.

Lithuanian eyewitnesses described how they were taken into the enclosure of the fort and told to undress and proceed to a shower room. Instead, they were led to the edge of deep pits, then beaten and pushed until they fell in. From the edge of dugouts, the Lithuanian militia then opened fire with automatic weapons. Anybody who was still alive after the machine gunning was over was killed with single shots. Their belongings and discarded clothing were taken to the Gestapo headquarters for sorting. Some of it was done by the Jewish brigade employed by the Gestapo. Throughout November and December, thousands of

Jews from western Europe marched past the ghetto to their execution. Quietly and obediently, they walked towards Fort IX, never doubting the promises of the Nazis.

The Jewish council kept insisting that the only way of avoiding the fate of the Jews from west Europe was by cooperation with the German authorities and by putting the whole ghetto labour force at their disposal. There was no problem finding volunteers for the jobs in town, but the Jewish police had to resort to force in order to ensure a sufficient supply of workers for the back-breaking shift work at the airport.

As soon as the workers settled in their workplace, they began a desperate search for food and fuel, but it took the best part of winter and a high toll in life before they managed to establish contact with Lithuanian friends willing to help, and with black marketeers prepared to trade.

At the end of November the temperature dropped below zero and kept dropping. Even before the frost set in, the ghetto was stripped of every combustible item and there was hardly any fuel left for cooking or heating. The winter of 1941-42 was one of the most severe on record and the population, which was already weakened by hunger, had now to face a new menace – hypothermia.

I found it easy to collect timber, but very difficult to acquire food. Occasionally, I managed to beg or steal a pocketful of potatoes, but it was a risky undertaking. It was easier to scrounge potato peel – which was quite filling – but no matter how well it was cleaned and prepared, it left a bitter taste. There was plenty of timber scattered around the building sites of the Heeresbau; the trouble was that it was frozen solid. I had to chop it up quickly during lunchbreaks and carry it four or five miles through ice and snow to the ghetto.

We had then to face checks and searches at the gates. Fortunately, the Lithuanian guards could be bribed to turn a blind eye, as long as there were no Germans about. In the morning, on leaving for work, we were usually informed by the Jewish police whether it was a safe day for bringing in provisions. Their advice was quite reliable, but on a few occasions the usual guards were replaced by new recruits, and all our food and firewood were confiscated by the eager young partisans.

In the middle of the winter 1941-42, we had to move house. The ghetto boundaries were reduced to allow the Lithuanians to move in. Our new place was even more overcrowded than the old one, but we managed to install an old-fashioned iron stove. It was the height of luxury. With my supply of firewood, we could cook and keep ourselves a bit warmer. One day that winter, posters appeared ordering us to surrender our fur coats. The Jewish police set up a fur collection centre, and the coats were duly handed over.

Heeresbau

My work for the Heeresbau, sketching and measuring army barracks, continued all winter. The cold inside the abandoned buildings was as bad as in the open, but the work was easy. About three hours a day were spent marching to work and back, but nobody was chasing us; we could take it easy. The German and Lithuanian supervisors were reasonable people, unlike the supervisors at the airport. The Jewish kapos at the Heeresbau were the leading civil and construction engineers of Kaunas, always helpful and considerate. Even our guards, mostly Ukrainians, were a lot more friendly than the guards at the airport.

The harassment came from higher up, from the soldier in charge of supervising the Ukrainians and the Heeresbau work brigades. He was Obergefreiter (Lance–Corporal) Sorets, an ambitious, aggressive and highly excitable Austrian. We called him 'Scheissegal Sorets' because of his favourite expletive, "Das ist mir scheissegal!" (I don't give a shit!).

Every morning at the ghetto gate, his ranting and raving,

which could be heard above the general tumult, ensured that in the scramble for workers, he could always have priority over the other German employers. He lasted about a year, mercilessly bullying not only us but also the Ukrainian and German soldiers under his command.

He was replaced by a gentle and friendly man, Sergeant Müller, who informed us that Sorets had managed to get promoted to the rank of sergeant and had been promptly sent to the Russian front. Then he added with a smirk, "I don't think that he'll be missed."

The man in charge of the engineering and maintenance department was a civil engineer, Sergeant Wagner, a decent, compassionate human being, determined to help us as much as possible. He was, however, outranked by a sergeant-major, a fanatical Nazi who did not tolerate any deviation from the party line. Everybody was terrified of him – the Jews, the Lithuanians and the Germans. His usual punishment for the Jews was a beating, delivered in person; for the Germans – a transfer to the front.

The sergeant-major became aware of Wagner's attitude to the Jews and had him transferred. But before he left, he informed uncle Mike that there had been a determined effort by the local Nazi administration and German enterprises to halt the killing of Jews. They had sent a number of petitions to Berlin pointing out that, in view of the shortage of skilled labour, it would be of benefit to the German economy to exploit the ghetto workers instead of eliminating them. Wagner was not too optimistic about the outcome of the petitions. He believed that the head of the SS, Reichsführer Himmler, and the leading Nazi ideologists were too obsessed with the idea of a Judenfrei (Jew-free) Europe to let economic considerations stand in their way. It was a year later, when news of the systematic extermination of Polish Jews reached us, that we realised how right he had been. After the departure of our protector, the drawing department was disbanded, but we were all re-employed by the plumbing and maintenance section of the Heeresbau.

On 6 February 1942, 500 Jews were deported to Riga. Initially, the Jewish police tried to round up the people from lists prepared by the Jewish council. They met with such resistance that they had to give up, and the job was completed by the Germans in the usual, brutal manner. The 500 were taken to Riga for slave labour; only a handful survived the extremely difficult conditions.

The Wannsee Conference

In January 1942, at Wannsee near Berlin, a secret conference of Nazi chiefs took place to confirm the fate of the Jews. The plan outlined implementation of 'The Final Solution of the Jewish Question', no matter how irreplaceable the Jewish labour, and no matter how damaging to the war effort. The method of mass shootings used in eastern Europe was considered too slow and primitive. No cost or effort was to be spared in introducing more efficient ways to kill eight million Jews under German control. Gas chambers had to be built, crematoria erected, a transportation network laid on. A whole industry of death had to be created. Destruction of life was to become an end in itself.

We knew nothing about it, but we observed all around us the self-defeating results of blind fanaticism. In the Soviet-occupied parts of eastern Europe, at the beginning of the war, the hatred of Communism was so strong that the German conquerors were greeted as liberators, and many eastern nations joined in the fight against the Soviet power. However, the poison of the 'master race' ideology stood in the way of common sense. The eastern nations soon realised what it meant to be classed as inferior Slavic races, and became hostile towards the Nazis.

Spring and Summer 1942

The end of the exceptionally cold winter was greeted with relief by the ghetto population, especially since the food and fuel shortage began to ease. The improvement was due to the town workers' determination to take advantage of a multiplicity of new, favourable circumstances. These included the chaotic conditions created by the spring thaw, the relaxation of supervision – in no small measure due to a judicious use of bribery – the replacement of young indoctrinated guards by middle-aged soldiers, and the emergence of a country-wide black market economy. These changes created a unique but also risky opportunity to acquire provisions which were vital for the survival of the ghetto population, and it was our Heeresbau brigade which was well placed to exploit it.

It seemed that nature was on our side. Owing to the keen frost, the water pipes, the mains supply, even the lagged boilers and central heating systems used to heat the large buildings in town, froze solid. They burst and when the thaw came, it released a flow of water which damaged everything in its path. For us it was a reassuring sight. The fact was that the Jews had a virtual monopoly of the plumbing and central heating trade, and it was our brigade which had the expertise to repair the giant sectional cast iron boilers. There was enough work for our plumbers, engineers, electricians, carpenters and builders to last for years. Our first task was to effect emergency repairs to military hospitals, buildings requisitioned by the German authorities and army barracks which were scattered all over town. We moved around so much that it was not easy to enforce orders to keep us constantly under armed guard. Now was our chance to reap the benefits of our efforts, expended during autumn and winter, to establish contact with Lithuanian friends and set up connections with the black market traders of Kaunas.

The Lithuanian population who had welcomed and collaborated with the German army had expected to be rewarded with political independence. Instead, they had to watch in anger the abolition of their provisional government and the imposition of direct rule. Realising that the true aim of the Nazis was the exploitation of the country, the leaders of Lithuania established an underground resistance movement which managed to attract widespread support. Part of an expression of mass defiance was the emergence of a country-wide black economy which, despite drastic countermeasures by the Gestapo, continued to flourish throughout the time of the German occupation. The mounting hostility to Nazi rule did not translate into any sympathy for the Jews, yet such was the attraction of acquiring quality goods at knock-down prices that black marketeers were prepared to face fearful risks in order to trade with the ghetto population. Our family was a case in point.

During the 'calm period' we traded in nine worsted suits, eight jackets, trousers, and other items of clothing and bedding. My contribution consisted of three worsted suits, three jackets and some trousers. We exchanged quality items for basic food supplies, mostly flour, bread and potatoes. The food was enough to keep us from starving, but not from being hungry. The profiteering was on a large scale, but we were in no position to bargain. It was common knowledge that the 14,000 murdered Jews had left behind a surplus of merchandise which was bound sooner or later to appear on the black market. We had our own profiteers – Jewish smugglers and speculators who took risks the ghetto population was either not able or not prepared to take. They reaped a generous reward, but they seldom lasted long enough to enjoy it. Every day, in broad daylight, we could see them walking on the pavement without the yellow Star of David. They were running the risk of being recognised by many of the Lithuanian or Ukrainian guards walking the streets of Kaunas. Some of the soldiers looked the other way. Others did not.

Our team leader, a young central heating engineer, decided to emulate them. One day, as he was walking on the pavement without his yellow patches, he ran straight into one of our guards.

He was arrested and shot by the Gestapo.

The rest of the Heeresbau workers, including myself, also managed to benefit from the illegal trade, but we chose to use a safer, more cumbersome method. We also walked unaccompanied through town, but the difference was that we marched in the gutter as Jews were not allowed to walk on the pavement. We kept our yellow patches on, we carried a large tool of the trade, and just in case we were questioned, we always had a pre-arranged excuse. The illegal merchandise was in a shoulder bag, hidden under a variety of plumbing parts. It was a nerve-racking procedure, but fortunately the black marketeers were as safety conscious as we were. Some close shaves were unavoidable but on the whole we were quite happy with our efforts, until suddenly one morning we were ordered by our kapo to stop all our illegal activities. He explained that two young German soldiers in charge of the Lithuanian and Ukrainian guards were complaining about a breakdown of discipline and slackness at work, and were threatening to inform the sergeant-major. Our kapo deduced from their behaviour that the time was ripe for a judicious application of bribery. He installed a highly skilled and inventive silversmith-jeweller in his office and asked him to produce two rings with the initials of the soldiers. Despite being made from cheap raw materials, they looked magnificent. The Germans accepted the rings and ordered two more for their girlfriends. The crisis was over and we resumed our usual activities. The two soldiers did not last long. They were soon replaced by a friendly, middle-aged lance-corporal.

Meanwhile the silversmith-jeweller, who was officially employed as a welder, was busy turning out rings, brooches, earrings and other ornamental jewellery of little intrinsic value, but of beautiful appearance. Business began to boom and bribery became a matter of routine. Quite a number of our supervisors and lower-ranked guards, including Sorets, received the initialled rings and placed orders for the folks back home.

I worked with the plumbers and heating engineers, repairing

and replacing central heating systems and converting school buildings into hospitals. The Heeresbau was continuously trying to get more Jewish workers and, owing to the energetic intervention of Sorets, they usually succeeded. By the end of summer 1942, they finished up with more than 800 workers.

Although we were under the administration of the German civil authorities, our true masters were the infernal twins, the SS and the Gestapo. They were constantly finding new ways of humiliating and harassing us. In May, an order was issued to terminate all pregnancies. Then another order followed – to close down all schools and synagogues. The claustrophobic atmosphere within the ghetto depressed me. Every morning I was glad to leave for work and every evening I was reluctant to return. Still, to keep our sanity, we pretended that it was possible to live a normal life in abnormal circumstances. We tried to socialise, to organise lectures and concerts. The Jewish council, taking advantage of the 'calm period', applied for permission to form an orchestra. It was granted, although performances of German music were banned. The orchestra was established and gave a number of concerts. At the time, I was working a long way from the ghetto. By the time I reached home, loaded with firewood and potatoes, I was too tired to go out.

Autumn Developments

We were left in relative peace until October 1942. Then came a demand for 370 workers for Riga. Lists were secretly prepared by the Jewish council and the Jewish police proceeded to round up the victims by force. On 18 November the ghetto had to witness a public hanging. A Jew had been caught trying to escape from the ghetto with false identity papers. The hanging was performed by a member of the Jewish police in the main square, and the body left to hang for 24 hours. On the day of the hanging I was transferred to a sign-writing job at a Hitler Youth Training Centre in Panemune, near Kaunas. Having witnessed the behaviour of the teenage fanatics at the airport, I was apprehensive about my new job, but I soon discovered that I need not have worried.

The chief of the centre was a veteran party member, an SA (Stürmabteilung/Storm Troopers) officer from East Prussia, called Koch. He was a crafty old trooper who knew that to keep his safe and cushy job, he had to turn the teenagers into model soldiers. And he achieved it by bullying, by relentless drilling and by a Prussian-type discipline which he called "kadaverge-horsam", blind obedience (literally, carcass obedience). He used his wicked sense of humour to mock, intimidate or sometimes dazzle his charges, but his most frightening weapon was his booming voice. Once or twice, after thoroughly bawling out the boys, he turned to me with a smirk and said, "Gut gebrüllt was?" (Didn't I shout well?). The drill sergeants shared their chief's passion for discipline, but not his wit. This was just as well because, besides being selected for their bullying abilities, they were required to indoctrinate their charges with the ideology of the master race. As for the boys, there was none of the carefree, boisterous behaviour associated with teenagers. It was difficult to believe that these gloomy, meek and docile creatures could be turned into merciless killers.

I was well treated by Koch and his staff. He helped me with food, kept me on as long as he could, and assigned to me some of his charges whose help I needed to put up the signs. I was in charge and the youngsters had to follow my orders. There were some Russian POWs engaged in gardening and maintenance. They looked well and, as far as I could see, were well treated.

Retribution for Stalingrad

Our Lithuanian contacts kept us well informed about the progress of the war. Up to the autumn of 1942, the news of German advances did not fill us with any hope. There was better news in the winter of 1942. The Germans had been beaten back at Stalingrad and were facing encirclement by the Red Army. On 2 February 1943, when the trapped German 6th Army under General Paulus surrendered, the scale of the Soviet victory exceeded our expectations.

In January 1943, with the situation in Stalingrad deteriorating, the mood of the Germans was becoming ugly. In the streets of Kaunas, Jews were arrested and beaten up on the slightest pretext. Especially dangerous were the young SS men who fully believed the Nazi propaganda that all Jews were part of an evil 'Jewish-Bolshevik' conspiracy.

At the time, I was working in the centre of town. Being well aware of the tense situation, I took great care never to talk to a civilian, or to step on the pavement or into a public place, always to wear the two yellow Stars of David and always to remove my cap at the sight of a military uniform.

One morning, at the end of January, as I was walking in the gutter of a busy main road, I failed to notice a young SS man who was approaching on the pavement. With a mighty blow he knocked off my cap and began hitting me. I stood petrified, fearing that he would shoot me, but after he had beaten me up, his anger seemed to subside and he screamed, "You Jews deserve to be shot for plunging us into war; now apologize and run before I do you in." A feeling of relief and even gratitude replaced the paralysing fear of death. I mumbled an apology and, terrified that his display of magnanimity might be short-lived, ran away as fast as I could.

I was lucky to be spared. A few days later, on 3 February 1943, a day after the surrender of the 6th Army, 48 Jews were picked up on the streets of Kaunas and at the ghetto gates. They were savagely beaten, taken to Fort IX and shot. This ritual seemed to satisfy the need for revenge. Shocked by the killings, but encouraged by the first major German defeat, the ghetto settled back to the usual routine.

Encounters at Work

Shortly after the Stalingrad surrender, I had a conversation with an elderly quartermaster-major. We had just finished discussing the repairs required to his central heating when, pointing to my yellow star, he said, "I have been here long enough to know what's going on, although not many in Germany know it." Then he explained to me that the present battles were only the beginning, that the war would develop on two fronts, resulting in a long and terrible slaughter, but one thing was certain – and he pointed again at my star of David – "the aftermath for us Germans will be even worse than the war."

My work at the Heeresbau, at the army hospitals, convalescent homes and barracks meant that I met lots of German soldiers, nurses, doctors and technicians. This was the conventional, ordinary face of Germany, very different from the brutal Nazi administration of the ghetto.

The hospitals were full of casualties from the eastern front, undergoing treatment or recuperating before going home. The early jingoistic euphoria had completely evaporated. Most of the soldiers were deeply affected by the savagery of the fighting. There was a lot of grumbling and scepticism. Some were openly cynical and hostile towards the Nazi leadership and the war, but no matter how war-weary and disappointed, their deeply-ingrained belief in obedience and discipline was not affected. There was also a minority of hard-line, dedicated Nazis, mostly among the younger soldiers.

One of the buildings I worked in was previously the German school. It was a strange feeling to walk into the classrooms where I had spent four years of my life, and to see row upon row of beds with wounded, burned soldiers swathed in bandages.

A couple of blocks away, the Russian school building had been converted into a convalescent home for severely maimed Ukrainians who fought on the German side. They were the dregs of humanity, despised and neglected by their German masters, and cut off from their own people. The only cheerful man amongst the gloom was the staff sergeant in charge, a lively, optimistic Berliner who was struggling on, without nursing staff, without even the basic facilities.

Despite our large team of electricians, plumbers, carpenters and heating engineers, we only managed the emergency work. The pleading of the staff sergeant did not move the Heeresbau as we were transferred to a more urgent job. This new job was to repair the broken-down central heating system in a building about half a mile from my pre-war place of residence. It was a three-storey house of six flats converted to a German army brothel.

The man in charge was an easygoing Lithuanian who kept an eye on the girls, but who could not care less about our work schedules. We managed to make the repairs last two weeks by pretending to find new faults. The reason for our efforts to extend the stay was nothing to do with the girls themselves; rather, it was the regular supply of food that they provided. They must have felt empathy with fellow pariahs, since they took some considerable risks to provide us with bread, potatoes and cigarettes. Most of it was smuggled into the ghetto – together with a sizeable quantity of condoms, which, unlike the food, were there for the asking.

At lunchtime on the first day, while the girls were fooling around, a tall, handsome woman came over to me and, after making sure that we were not overheard, she disclosed the reason for her approach. She had worked for a number of years as a domestic for a Jewish family called Friedman, a married couple with two children. By a strange coincidence they had lived in one of the top floor flats of the building we were now working in. She had left the Friedmans to get married and moved to a provincial town. In the winter of 1941, after her marriage broke up, she became destitute, returned to Kaunas and finished up in the brothel. Her efforts to trace the Friedmans were in vain and now she wanted me to make enquiries about them in the ghetto.

I agreed to her request, but pointed out that well over half the Jewish population had been massacred. After some searching, I established that the family had been a victim of the 'selection' of 4 October 1941. That was the 'Small Ghetto Action', when only bearers of the Jordan 'lifesaver' passes were released and allowed to cross to the main ghetto. As an airport worker, Friedman did not have a pass and the family were amongst the 1,500 people who were taken to Fort IX and executed.

Despite my warning not to build up too many hopes, the woman was deeply shocked by the tragic news. She dissolved into tears, bemoaning the fate of her former employer as well as her present sorry and demeaning occupation. After regaining her composure, she declared her determination to leave the brothel at the first opportunity. Then, to my amazement, she explained that all she had to do to free herself was to accept one of the man marriage proposals she was getting from her steady German customers. To our chagrin, all the future repair and maintenance work at the brothel was allocated to Lithuanian craftsmen and we never went there again.

Contacts with the Outside World

During the spring and summer of 1943, the demand for Jewish labour was increasing. Besides a large thriving ghetto workshop which provided work for carpenters, locksmiths, tailors and shoe-makers, thus increasing their food rations, there were 200 outside work brigades of about 5,000 workers, bringing in some food and fuel, and keeping open the window to the outside world. We were well-informed about the set-backs for the Germans on the Russian front and about the aerial bombardments of Germany. The treatment of the Russian POWs improved, a sign that the Soviets were capturing a lot of Germans. In Kaunas, the German police started rounding up Lithuanians for forced labour and army service.

Disturbing news was reaching us from Poland about gas chambers and the genocide of Jews and Gypsies. This news upset our new hopes that because of the desperate shortage of workers, we might be spared. Meanwhile, some Jews started building hiding places – behind false walls, inside cellars or attics – to escape any future selections or 'actions'. Some, desperate to save their children, managed to smuggle them out of the ghetto and to hand them over to friendly Lithuanians.

Some grown-ups also managed to find hiding places in town or in the countryside. My cousin Irena, daughter of Auntie Sonia, and my two cousins, Margaret and Alick, Uncle George Strom's children, left the ghetto. They survived the war thanks to the dedication of Lithuanians who hid them and looked after them, despite the risk of discovery and summary execution. That was the fate of a Jewish girl, a classmate of mine, and her Lithuanian boyfriend. He tried to hide her in his flat in Kaunas, but the neighbours denounced them to the Gestapo. Some escapees found it impossible to stay in their hiding places and had to return to the ghetto.

Before cousin Irena left us to go into hiding, our grandmother, who was suffering from high blood pressure, died peacefully in her sleep. At the time it was a blow to all of us, but only half a year later we realised what a blessing it was to die a natural death.

The End of the 'Calm Period'

The relative calm of the ghetto was disrupted in October 1943 by a change at the top. The SA yielded command of the ghetto to the SS. We knew that the huge concentration camp system was run by the SS. Could our ghetto be on the list to be converted into a concentration camp? It was a frightening prospect.

On a cold autumn day, returning from work, I had my first

taste of the new set-up. We noticed that the searches were stricter than usual, and that there were quite a lot of SS men at the gate. When my turn came, a short, stocky SS officer appeared from the police station, called me over and started to search me from head to toe. First of all, I had to take off my shoulder bag and put it on the floor. Then my cap was pulled inside out and minutely examined. He took my scarf, carefully running his fingers along it, feeling every crease. I had to take off my coat, jacket, trousers and shoes. As I was watching this detailed and thorough procedure, my fright turned into incomprehension. Was he demonstrating how to conduct a proper search, or did he think I was a spy hiding a microfilm?

He did not find anything and left with his bodyguard as suddenly as he had appeared. A Jewish policeman, who was a friend of mine, helped me gather my belongings and took me to the nearest shelter. As I started dressing, he explained to me that the SS officer was Obersturmbannführer (Colonel) Goecke, the 'butcher of Riga' and now the man in charge of the ghetto. He added, "It was a weird search; he could have been looking for money. It's a good job you were clean."

I opened the side pocket of my shoulder bag and showed him a bundle of money. He shook his head in amazement, "One look into your bag and you would have been a 'goner'. Now, a word of warning: the smuggling days are over, our cosy arrangement with the Lithuanian guards is finished! They are too scared of the new bosses from the SS."

We felt that the arrival of Goecke and his henchmen meant trouble and we were right. On the morning of 26 October 1943, after the workers left the ghetto, the Jewish police started rounding up people from lists prepared by the Jewish council. The resistance was fierce; the Germans lost their patience with the inefficiency of the Jewish police and decided to bring in the Lithuanian and Ukrainian militia. After prolonged and ferocious beatings, they managed to force over 3,000 Jews into lorries and take them away. Children were torn away from their families and men and women separated, and taken for slave labour to Estonia. We found out later that the children were gassed in Auschwitz.

Hard on the heels of what became known as the 'Estonia Action' came another blow: Goecke announced that the ghetto would be broken up into a number of concentration camps. The 1,500 airport workers would be housed in barracks near their place of work. The Heeresbau workers would go to Sanciai, a suburb of Kaunas. The rest would stay in a reduced area of the ghetto. The Jewish council was given the task of planning and organising the move.

We knew that a change to concentration camp status meant primitive conditions, a strict regime and the segregation of men and women. But what frightened us most was news of a terrible 'action' in the ghetto of Siauliai, about 70 miles from Kaunas. According to reliable information, all the children under 12, all the sick and all those over 55 were forcibly removed from the ghetto.

As the ghetto desperation increased, so did the rate of escapes, organised mostly by the members of the underground resistance movement. Some of them were caught and shot, others taken for slave labour to Fort IX, but a small group managed to reach the forests of the Lithuanian countryside and start a fighting unit.

Not only the Jews were getting rattled, but also the Nazis. The bombing of Germany was getting more deadly. In Italy the Allied Forces were at the gates of Rome, and the Russians were approaching Poland, taking thousands of German prisoners. Maybe there was an end in sight to this madness.

Escape from Fort IX

In September 1943, the Nazis decided that it was time to destroy the evidence of the mass murders in Fort IX. Huge bonfires were lit, fuelled by petrol and timber, and the corpses were placed on top. Day and night, the ghetto was saturated with the sickening smell of burning flesh. The work was done by Russian POWs and by the captured groups of the ghetto underground movement. They were kept in escape-proof cells and continuously watched by Lithuanian and German guards. Yet some managed to escape. It was the only mass breakout from Fort IX. A number of them were recaptured and killed, but a small group of Jews secretly reached the ghetto and went into hiding. They could not risk endangering the ghetto inhabitants; as soon as they had told their story and recovered from their ordeal, they left for the second time for the forests of Lithuania.

They told a story of unbelievable courage and determination. Not long after their first escape from the ghetto, they were intercepted by the Lithuanian militia and handed over to the Gestapo. Despite torture and intensive interrogation, they did not disclose the secrets of their organisation. All this happened at the time when the Nazis took the decision to eliminate the evidence of the massacres in Fort IX. The execution of the escapees was postponed as all available manpower was required for the incineration of the bodies. As soon as the Jews arrived at the fort, they were put to work to recover the corpses from the pits and put them on bonfires. They calculated that there were approximately 60,000 bodies – mothers with babes in arms, children, men and women, some naked, some fully dressed. From the documents still in their pockets and from other clues, they established that besides the victims of our ghetto, there were the bodies of the west European Jews and of thousands of Russian POWs. With the help of a team of Russian-Jewish POWs who had been there over two years and who knew the fort's exact layout, they devised a plan of escape. Fortunately, they had a pool of skilled specialists: joiners, carpenters, locksmiths and engineers.

They had nothing to lose; everyone knew that sooner or later every prisoner would be shot. They scoured the pockets of the victims, and every metal object (pocket knives, keys, etc) was used to fashion primitive tools, drills, duplicate keys.

The break-out took place at Christmas 1943, the most suitable time, when the guards were full of food and booze. All the prisoners escaped and then split up. The group heading for the ghetto reached their destination, but the other group heading for the forests was not so lucky. Many of them were captured and killed.

Waldemar Ginsberg, 1938, Kaunas, age 17

In Kulautuva, Lithuania, 1937

Leaders of the Jewish Community (Kehilla) in Kaunas 1932

*On holiday with Mother and two friends at
Palanga on the Baltic Sea*

*Jewish sports group of the Association of Lithuanian Jews
in Israel gather in Kaunas 1935 under the banner of
Hapoel. Political and Zionist organisations, such as these,
were active in Lithuania.*

Vegetable market in Lithuania-Vilnius before the war

Pogrom in Kaunas. Lithuanian citizens help the Nazis kill Jews

*Jewish residents of Kaunas move wood
into the ghetto*

*Dr. Elkes is seen here in the Bikur Holim Jewish hospital with
some of his staff in 1933. He would later become leader of the
Jewish Council in Kaunas*

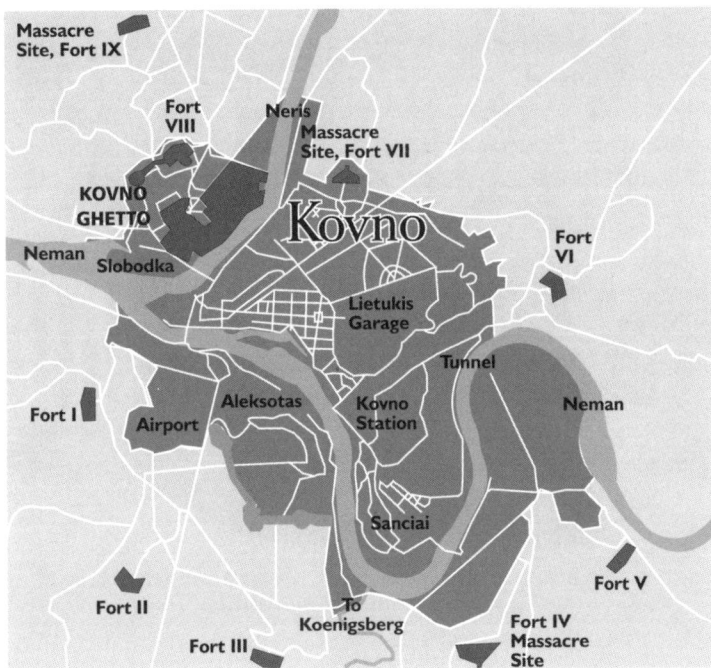

Kaunas

The flat were we lived before the war. First window, bottom floor, was my room. (Picture taken in 1987)

Food is hidden in the Kaunas ghetto. Thousands of Jews hid in bunkers. Most were discovered.

Boy working at a machine in the Kaunas ghetto workshop

Children in the Kaunas ghetto.

Prisoners in Dachau concentration camp

CHAPTER FOUR

THREATENING
DEVELOPMENTS

THE CONCENTRATION
CAMP IN KAUNAS

Concentration Camp Sanciai

In November 1943, the first transport of 1,500 Jews moved into
the concentration camp near the airport. A month later, it was
our turn. There were five of us: Grandpa, Mother, my stepfather,
Uncle Mike and I. Cousin Irene was in hiding, and my grandmother had since been laid to rest in the ghetto cemetery. We left
the ghetto subdued and depressed, taking with us a few bundles
of bedding and clothing. As soon as our lorry drove into the
camp, we realised that we were trapped in a proper prison, a
central square surrounded by makeshift wooden barracks.
Armed Ukrainian guards were watching us from behind a double
row of barbed wire. After a roll-call and careful headcount by the
SS and guards, we were allowed to retire to the barracks, where
the straw-covered, two-tiered bunks served for sleeping, eating
and storage. Although men and women were in separate
barracks, there was no ban on communication. We were allowed
to eat together and visit each other until bedtime.

After the morning roll-call and counting out at the departure gate, I was glad to leave the camp to go back to the familiar sights of leaking water pipes, burst boilers and radiators, and hospitals overflowing with casualties from the carnage on the eastern front. We also managed to scrounge some food and smuggle it into the camp to supplement our meagre rations.

Inside the camp, the pecking order developed in a similar way to the one in the ghetto, allowing for the reduced circumstances and opportunities in a smaller place. The ruling clique consisted of the same people who had wielded power in the ghetto. They looked healthy and well-fed. It was obvious that the system of power and privilege was self-perpetuating and that it was exploited for personal advantage – easier work, extra food, better accommodation and so on.

Shortly after our move to Sanciai, I was sent to do some central heating repairs in an army building in the centre of town, near the flat of the Lithuanian couple called Strimaitis who had arranged the hiding place for Irena. Despite the risk involved, I decided to visit them in order to find out how my cousin was faring, and to quiz Strimaitis, an ex-army officer, about the political situation. After assuring me that Irena was in safe hands, he provided me with a wealth of information. His view – that the defeat of Germany was a foregone conclusion, and it was in no small measure due to the Nazi obsession with the dogma of racial superiority – was not novel. It was also the view widely held by many among both Jewish and Gentile population. But his disclosures of the follies of Nazi rule, of chaotic conditions within their command structure and of rivalry between the ruling bodies were not well-known and made for fascinating listening.

He argued that of all the 'half-baked' doctrines of Nazi ideology, the most damaging to the war effort was the 'master race' theory. It was responsible for the policy of murder, pillage and exploitation which changed the attitude of the population from gratitude and friendship to hostility. Even more harmful was the continued interference in local decisions by the armchair ideologues in Berlin, who knew nothing about conditions in the occupied territories. It not only created confusion and conflict, but it also hindered the plans of the Wehrmacht (the German army) and the local Nazi authorities to recruit millions of Slav and Baltic volunteers who could have influenced the outcome of the war.

However, the question which troubled me most was how these developments would affect our chances of survival. Strimaitis was of the opinion that the SS was determined to continue with the 'Final Solution' regardless of the military circumstances, and that the transfer of Jewish prisoners from the ghetto to concentration camps was a move to facilitate its aims. Despite the good news about cousin Irena, I left the flat gripped by fear and foreboding.

The 'Children's Action'

Ever since the November news of the terrible 'Children's Action' in the ghetto of Siauliai, there was a nagging fear about the fate of the non-productive members of our camp. The three months of uneventful camp life had dulled some of our anxieties, but the worry about the security of our children was still deeply felt.

The children, mature beyond their years through the abnormal conditions of ghetto life, were unusually serious and well-behaved. They were the negation of the concept of prison life; they were the symbol, the reminder of normal conditions. They were always well looked after; no matter how severe the food shortage, they were getting their fill, and no matter how deep our worry was, we took care to shelter them from it. The only obvious sign of our anxiety was the fervour of prayers for the children's safety and the odd furtive tear during the blessing of the babies.

In our barracks, we were especially fond of the three Burstein boys whose carefree patter and smiling faces never failed to cheer us up. Every evening, led by their mother, they would march into our barracks, looking like three little angels – well-groomed, curly blond hair and large blue eyes. Despite the difference in their ages – the youngest was about two, the oldest seven or eight – they looked like peas in a pod.

On 27 March 1944 our brigade returned from work early. There was a strange, frightening silence over the camp; no children to greet us, not a soul to be seen in the whole compound. Full of foreboding, we waited for the counting to finish and rushed into the barracks. Our worst fears were confirmed. The children, the elderly, the sick and disabled were gone, snatched away in the most brutal manner by a detachment of Ukrainian militia, leaving behind the shocked and beaten-up camp workers who tried to resist.

I started looking for Grandpa. It was in vain. I found only his belongings scattered around his bunk. Our camp was small – only 1,200 people – and we all knew each other. As the workers started arriving, the panic, the frenzy increased. It was like a seething cauldron, people running around in all directions, searching, screaming, crying and sobbing uncontrollably. For a long time this persisted. Some were seized with hysteria, some with impotent rage, others with paralysing numbness. As darkness fell, the first shock was over, but the night was punctuated by cries, sobs and screams. And Kaunas wept.

This outrage of 27 March 1944 and the resulting trauma remains one of my most haunting memories to this day. All the hopes built up during the so-called 'calm period' had been shattered. We were back in the nightmare world of perverted Nazi morality, where it was a commendable action to kill the defenceless and a capital crime to shelter them. To me it seemed impossible that after this outrage the camp could ever return to its former routine. I believed that our passivity would stop, that the following day would be full of trouble and unrest, and that the grief-stricken workers would be too resentful and defiant to present themselves for work. I was wrong; I should have remembered the aftermath of the 'Big Action'. I also underestimated the amazing human capacity to absorb blow after blow and still continue the fight for survival.

In the morning, despite the despondency and defiance, the kapos and guards managed to assemble the brigades and send them to work. The main driving force was not the threat of the kapos and guards; it was the urge to survive, the necessity to find extra food, which was only obtainable outside the camp. We kept remembering the Soviet POWs – young, trained soldiers, dropping like flies because of the effects of starvation.

A few days after we resumed work, some Lithuanians informed us that there had been mass executions in a deep ravine outside Kaunas. Our camp presented a picture of utter gloom and despair. The silence of the graveyard had replaced the wailing and crying. Everywhere I looked there were reminders of the tragedy, the desperate look in mothers' eyes, the people moving around sullen and withdrawn, the Burstein couple numb with shock, sitting on the floor, lost in their private world of grief.

For the Heeresbau brigades, the work in town was getting more dangerous and difficult. The Germans and Lithuanians were rattled by the advance of the Red Army, which was rapidly approaching the borders of Lithuania. The German army's losses were running into millions, defeat was staring them in the face, and the Nazis were getting more vicious than usual. The German-Lithuanian honeymoon was long over. By now it was clear to everybody that the Nazis' true aim was not the liberation but the exploitation, plunder and colonisation of Lithuania. The leaders of the country, who tried to resist the despoliation and round-ups of young men for slave labour or army service, were arrested and sent to concentration camps in Germany. The response of the population varied. Some escaped to the safety of the countryside and some, fearing the Communists more than the Nazis, prepared to flee to Germany.

The situation in Kaunas was very tense. The town was full of SS and Gestapo agents and we had to be extremely careful. The first mistake was the last. There was no second chance.

The arrests of Jews were becoming more frequent. Some were trapped in the round-ups, some discovered in their hiding places, and some caught while bartering or buying food. They were taken to Fort IX, but instead of being shot, they were used to exhume and burn the bodies of the massacred Jews.

A couple of days after the 'Children's Action', we found out that the other camps had experienced similar horrors. The ghetto, which had meanwhile been reduced in size and changed to concentration camp status, fared even worse than we did. On the morning of 27 March, Goecke arrived with a large contingent of militia, lined up the Jewish police and took them to Fort IX. There they were interrogated under torture about the underground resistance movement and the hiding places. Forty of them refused to talk and were shot; ninety were returned to the ghetto and placed under the direct control of the Gestapo. They were, however, ostracised. There was the suspicion that they were released because they cooperated with the Gestapo. The searches and selections lasted two days. Hundreds of SS men and Ukrainians, with the help of vicious Alsatian dogs, searched every house from top to bottom, looking for children, invalids and old people. They broke open furniture, demolished walls and partitions, trying to find the hideouts. Any resistance was crushed by severe beating or by shooting.

Spring of 1944 saw the introduction of a lot of changes. The able-bodied personnel of the Heeresbau were required as cannon fodder on the eastern front, and were replaced by elderly incapacitated people, who looked confused and ill at ease. This change meant that we lost our kind and friendly sergeant, Müller, who had been our works supervisor since 1942. He explained to us that he did not expect to survive long on the eastern front; his only chance was a Heimatschuss – a bullet wound – which would be his passport home.

An example of the desperate shortage of manpower was the appearance of elderly guards of World War One vintage. The soldier in charge was a sergeant, disabled by frostbite, a grumpy and embittered Rhinelander who cursed the war and the Nazis at every opportunity. The other two guards were privates from Silesia, an eastern province of Germany. One was tiny, about five feet tall; the other was frail-looking and very thin. Their Silesian dialect was unintelligible and it was practically impossible to communicate with them. The sergeant, who was not noted for his patience, developed a habit of mocking and teasing them, "Just look at these specimens of our...... master race! They don't even know their own language." Then he would continue, "Can anybody here provide a translation into German?" We could not oblige; the Silesian dialect was as strange to us as it was to the sergeant.

This mocking went on for quite a long time and the two privates seemed to take it in their stride. Then, one day, without any good reason, the undersized soldier went berserk. After one of our workers asked him to repeat an order, he grabbed his rifle and shot him dead. Just as he was about to discharge his second shot, the sergeant pounced, overpowered him and led him away after a struggle. We did not find out what happened to the private, but we knew that killing a Jew was of no consequence. If any punishment was due, it would be for resisting the sergeant.

The evacuation of hospitals and official buildings meant that our workload in town was decreasing, but the expansion of our camp workshop was absorbing the released labour force. In June 1944 it was becoming clear that the speed of the Russian advance would enable them to reach Kaunas by the end of summer. The Nazis could not leave us behind to bear witness to their deeds; on the other hand, there would not be enough time to kill 12,000 people and destroy the evidence. The gas chambers of Auschwitz were also in danger because the Russians were on the borders of Poland. Deportation to a German concentration camp seemed to be the most likely outcome.

One morning, when all brigades were stopped from leaving the camp, we realised that the days of our camp were numbered. To our amazement, the camp workshop kept expanding;

new machinery was arriving and had to be installed. All hands were switched to unloading, and soon our engineers were operating the new machines. The last crate arrived two days before the camp was evacuated. It was carefully unpacked and then, a day later, repacked just as carefully for transport to Germany. The last day in the camp was spent dismantling all the contents of the workshop, putting them into crates and loading them onto trucks.

On the morning of 8 July 1944, the announcement came. We were to be deported to work in Germany. Under heavy guard we were taken to a nearby railhead. There were attempts at escape, but most of them ended in tragedy. We were crammed into cattle trucks and the journey to Germany began. Next day, on arrival at Stutthof near Danzig, the next stage of our tragedy was enacted: men and women were separated. That was the last time I saw my mother. She was taken to the notorious concentration camp of Stutthof, to the last stage of her suffering. We carried on. It was a nightmare journey into the depths of Germany. Step by step we had lost our homes, our belongings, our families. Were we now going to lose our lives in German concentration camps?

CHAPTER FIVE

WINTER OF DEATH

THE CONCENTRATION CAMP OF DACHAU-LANDSBERG

Concentration Camp No.1 – Dachau, Landsberg am Lech

We disembarked at the rail stop of Kaufering, near Landsberg am Lech in southern Bavaria. Then we marched to our destination, Camp No. 1. Our long journey was over; we were prisoners in a branch of the concentration camp of Dachau, one of the oldest and largest in Germany. Dazed and fearful, we looked around at the forbidding watchtowers, the large searchlights, the electrified barbed wire, the SS guards with their Alsatian dogs.

The searches started straight away. We had to surrender all our belongings and exchange our shoes for wooden ones, our clothing for a striped prison uniform with a yellow triangle on the chest and back. The German kapo who was frisking me confiscated all my documents and photographs except for the picture of my mother. As he was handing it back to me, an SS man who was supervising the search intervened. "Don't give it back, it might give him the idea that he's still a human being." He took the picture of my mother and tore it up.

To confirm that I had become a nameless non-person, my camp identity number – 82336 – was sewn in below the yellow triangle. The conversion into proper Dachau prisoners was completed by shaving our heads. Now we looked like the rest of the camp inmates, although some of them were German criminals (green triangle on the left side of the chest), some homosexual (pink triangles), and some political (red).

The internal camp administration was entrusted to four chief kapos: two were German criminals and two Hungarian Jews whose privileged life depended on their willingness to bully the rest of us. It appeared that we would have a difficult existence ahead.

A day after our arrival in the camp, just as we were trying to settle in, the air raid siren sounded. An American fighter plane appeared suddenly out of a blue sky and swooped low over us. It was a joy to see our tormentors running in all directions like headless chickens. We just stood and cheered until the pilot opened fire. By the time we hit the ground, we had two casualties: one prisoner killed and one wounded. Despite the losses, the raid lifted our spirits. For prisoners who felt forgotten and abandoned, the sight of an American plane was a considerable morale boost. We were hoping and praying for another raid but it never came.

Working Conditions

The bombing of the German towns badly damaged their industry. The wooded area around Landsberg, 45 miles from Munich and 40 miles from Dachau, was ideal for locating the replacement underground factories. The concentration camp of Dachau could organise the slave labour; the river Lech could provide the water and gravel, and the woods the camouflage. Eleven camps were built to house the prisoners. It was an immense effort, a race against time which the Nazis could not win, but unfortunately it was the starving prisoners – me included – who were forced to join the race. The labour shortage was acute. Transports of new workers were arriving all the time – Russian POWs, men and women survivors of the ghetto of Siauliai, prisoners from various concentration camps, even survivors of Auschwitz.

The biggest construction site was a huge underground chamber to replace the bombed-out aeroplane factories of Messerschmitt. The contractor was the firm Moll, employing prisoners from Camps 1, 2 and 3. The work was back-breaking: feeding sand, gravel and cement into huge mixers and then transporting, pouring and levelling the concrete. My stepfather, uncle and I managed to get easier, more specialised work with the smaller subcontracting firm by the name of Lingemann, laying drains and sewers, electric cables, installing the network of pipes for the water supply. It was not as demanding as at Moll, and the supervisors were less brutal.

There was little shelter, the work was in the open, and with the approach of autumn, conditions became desperate. The flimsy camp garb did not keep out the cold, especially if it got wet. In addition to the eleven-hour shift, we had to stand for a long time during roll-call in the morning and in the evening, on the muddy and wet camp square. My feet were permanently wet. I knew that if I could not replace my leaking shoes, I would not last long. The warehouse kapo was a humane and friendly German with a pink triangle (homosexual). He let me pick a pair of new wooden-soled boots and even let me take a warm overcoat.

All that probably helped me to survive the winter, but the biggest problem by far was hunger. There was no possibility of extra food, as in Lithuania, and it was impossible to manage on a ration of 300 grams of bread and some watery soup. However, there was a minority which always had enough food, and it was nearly always the same minority. Despite the fact that some sort of pecking order was already in operation when we arrived in Camp No. 1, most of the members of our ruling clique still managed to secure the sort of cushy jobs they were holding down in the ghetto and concentration camps of Lithuania.

Undeserved privilege was a prominent and repelling feature of the Nazi prison system. But unlike in the ghettos and death camps, where even privileged prisoners could be killed, in the satellite camps of Dachau, the main killers were hunger, disease and back-breaking work. Any prisoners who managed to monopolise the cushy jobs in the kitchen, hospital or office had an easier life and a good chance of survival. Their sin was cunning and guile rather than brutality. The real villains who were feared and hated in equal measure were the small minority of inmates who used cunning and brutality to ingratiate themselves with their SS masters. They became part of the parallel system of camp authority that was wielded by the prisoners. Without their help, the concentration camp system could not have been sustained. They had bought their privileged position at a high cost. The rest of the prisoners regarded them as malevolent usurpers and hated them as much, if not more, than the SS.

Arrivals and Departures

In the autumn, a transport of Hungarian women arrived from Auschwitz. They looked half dead with their shaven heads, their clothes in tatters and their emaciated bodies. Amongst them was my future wife, but I did not know her in the camp. It was only after the liberation, when we met in a hospital, that we realised that we had been in the same camp and had worked on the same construction site.

The women were still in deep shock from their Auschwitz experiences. The Nazi terror came late to Hungary (spring 1944), but it came with a devastating suddenness. Whereas we served a three-year ghetto apprenticeship to prepare us for the ordeals of life in a concentration camp, the Hungarian Jews were torn from their near-normal life in the spring and summer of 1944 and taken straight to Auschwitz. There were nearly three-quarters of a million Jews in Hungary, and the death factories could not cope with such large numbers. At the same time, the other concentration camps were clamouring for more slave labour. After killing over a quarter of a million, including the old, the disabled, the children and their mothers, the Nazis transferred many of the able-bodied men and women from Auschwitz to various camps in Germany.

The cumulative effect of hunger, cold, dirt and back-breaking work in the open soon became apparent, especially amongst the Moll workers. The first sign of deterioration was a puffiness around the eyes. Then followed swelling of the legs and loss of weight and strength. The victims became slow and lethargic, walking skeletons or 'Musselmänner' as they were called in the camp. There was no hope for them; some died in the camp, some were picked out during the dreaded selections. Not only the Musselmänner, but also anyone looking old or haggard was put on a transport to the crematorium of Auschwitz. It was done very casually, by an SS man pointing his whip at anybody he did not consider fit for work.

My stepfather, who was a thin but healthy man, was unexpectedly picked out at such a selection. By the time Uncle Mike and I found out about it, he was already on the transport to Auschwitz. The worry now was the state of health of my uncle. He was very close to his older brother and lapsed into a state of deep depression. He was an intellectual, a gentleman of the old school, quite unable to adapt physically or mentally to the camp conditions.

Crime and Punishment

The system of keeping us in check was, very simply, terror. In its most basic and primitive form, it meant physical violence. Beating up a prisoner was immediately satisfying, cheap and effective. The other common punishment was 10-24 lashes on the bare buttocks, depending on the mood of the SS man or chief kapo, and on the nature of the crime.

For Sergeant Forster, however, the mere fact that we existed was a crime. On cold mornings, he used to warm up by picking out a prisoner and giving him a thorough beating. On the days of German defeats – which were nearly every day – the beatings were particularly vicious. I usually managed to avoid trouble by always being on my guard and trying to be as invisible and inaudible as possible. One day, however, I was not vigilant enough and paid the price. As I was leaving the toilet, I suddenly noticed that Forster was standing in front of me. He pushed me against the toilet wall and started to hit me. The only way to limit the damage was not to fall down too soon; his heavy boots could cause a lot more injuries than his fists. It was not easy, but I managed to stay upright until I felt that he was getting exhausted. When I fell down, he just gave me one kick and left.

There was another sergeant who was feared just as much as Forster; it was the camp commandant Kirsch, known as 'Napoleon'. He ordered and organised the public hanging of five Jews for the crime of 'destroying state property'. It was a crime of which we were all guilty. The flimsy striped uniform could not keep us warm, so we cut up our towels or blankets to make foot-wrappers or vests for protection against the cold. Some enterprising prisoners even managed to make trousers.

'Napoleon' Kirsch assembled the whole camp in front of the gallows. Even the women were brought over, but they were allowed to turn away at the moment of hanging. As was the custom, the bodies were left hanging for 24 hours. This punishment caused a panic among the prisoners, and they quickly got rid of incriminating evidence. So did I – by getting rid of two squares cut from my blanket, which I had used as foot-wrappers ever since my arrival at the camp, when I had surrendered my socks and had to have something to keep my feet warm.

Winter at Moll

The poor sanitary conditions and lack of facilities to keep ourselves and our garments clean were ideal for an invasion of lice. We were covered with them and much of our spare time was spent trying to shake them off. We used to sit at the end of our bunks with our shirts or jackets turned inside out, carefully picking up the lice and crushing them between our thumbnails. They used to burst with a satisfying click, but despite all our efforts, we could not stop the itching or reduce the invasion.

Lice were carriers of spotted fever and, just before the onset of winter, cases of the illness appeared. The infection was spreading fast. Our camp was quarantined – after the early shift left, the camp was sealed and nobody could get in or out. Uncle Mike, who was in the clinic at the time trying to recover from exhaustion, stayed in the camp. Our work brigade was not allowed to return. After the shift work with our plumbing firm Lingemann was finished, we were taken straight to Camp No. 3 near Kaufering, given a wash and new blankets. It was not much use. We did not receive any new garments and our own efforts at washing our lice-infested clothes ended in failure.

As we were trying to settle into our new barracks, our kapo informed us that our work with Lingemann was finished. We would remain in Camp No. 3 over winter and work for Moll. We were horrified. Our chances of surviving a winter at Moll were very slim indeed. As soon as we moved into Camp No. 3, we noticed a different atmosphere. The camp was smaller, more relaxed, the supervision less strict. The German sergeant in charge of the guards was an easygoing innkeeper from a neighbouring village. The searches were a formality, and we had no trouble bringing in enough firewood to keep our small iron stove going all night. We could dry our shoes and our clothes and keep warm, and the roll-calls were mercifully short. But all these advantages were cancelled out by the work at Moll. The eleven-hour nightshift was a killer – dirty, difficult work in freezing weather, and only one break to gulp down a bowl of watery soup.

The heaviest work was feeding the huge concrete-mixers, carrying the bags of cement, pushing the tipper wagons loaded to the brim, pouring and levelling the concrete. The noise was deafening, the air full of dirt and cement dust, the site a mixture of mud and cement. In overall charge was the ubiquitous Organisation Todt (OT) which was supervising Germany's construction and fortification work. I knew it well; it was the same OT which had driven us on without respite or mercy when we were working at the airport in Kaunas. The supervisors were as unpleasant there as they had been in Lithuania. The news of the rapid Russian and Allied advances towards Germany, and of the destruction of their country caused by the incessant bombardment, made them tense and short-tempered. So far as their job was concerned, that too was frustrating and depressing. They were up against shortages of building materials, chaos in the supply system, and a workforce so weakened by malnutrition that they were hardly able to move. The futility of the whole enterprise must have been clear to them. But they carried on with grim determination, never relaxing, driving us beyond our strength and endurance, and frequently venting their frustration on us. This combination of hard work and malnutrition was taking its toll. The number of Musselmänner was increasing. More and more prisoners were giving up the struggle, sinking into a cataleptic state. By then, death had already taken over, just waiting for the body to draw its last breath. There were no selections in Camp No. 3. The Musselmänner died in their own bunks, quietly, without fuss. In the morning, the bodies were placed on bogies, taken outside the perimeter of the camp and unceremoniously dumped into a shallow hole in the ground. Of course, under normal circumstances, this indifference to the deceased would have been deplored, but considering our prolonged exposure to the dehumanising effect of Nazi terror, it was not surprising that our emotional responses and moral sensibilities were somewhat stifled.

Red Cross Parcels

I was in such a state. I felt that I, too, was going to finish up as a Musselmann. I had reached the end of my endurance. I was becoming apathetic and depressed, preferring to retreat into a dream world rather than face reality. I had recurring visions of tucking in at a big table laden with food and then sleeping off the meal in a clean bed between crisp, white sheets. I was aware how dangerous it was to escape into a dream world, but I needed help to snap out of it. Quite out of the blue this help came in the form of an announcement that we were about to receive a Red Cross parcel of sugar and cigarettes. Initially, this statement was greeted with suspicion. Opinions were expressed that it was a mockery, a cruel joke, or even an attempt to poison us, but a couple of hours later, as we were tasting the sugar, as the cigarette smoke filled our barracks, the mood changed completely.

For the next few weeks, conversation concentrated on the significance of the parcels, which was considered as encouraging and promising, and on the therapeutic qualities of sugar. The conditions for a fireside chat were good. We had enough firewood to keep our barracks nice and warm. The only snag was that the warmth produced bouts of violent itching. So we usually took off our garments, turned them inside out, had a good scratch, and then started the routine I described previously: picking the lice one by one and squashing them between our thumbnails. Then the conversation on the properties of sugar would begin in earnest, punctuated by the reassuring clicks of the bursting lice. We would go on and on, until we convinced ourselves that sugar was the most nourishing and energising food, and that it was unique in promoting endurance and memory. After some prisoners became sick from eating too much sugar, we decided to ration ourselves to four to six lumps a day.

Another boost to our confidence was the information received from the German innkeeper. The Americans were approaching the Rhine; the Russians were pushing into Hungary and were near Danzig. That was the best news of all. It meant that the concentration camp of Stutthof, where the Jewish women were imprisoned, might soon be free. He also confirmed that the heavy air bombardment of Germany was sowing death and destruction and paralysing the war effort. We could well believe it. Day and night we could hear the roar of hundreds of bombers. On cloudless days, the gleaming four-engined aircraft were clearly visible, crossing the sky unhindered from horizon to horizon. The collapse of Germany seemed so near. If only we could last out a few more weeks!

Among some of us, the survival instinct grew stronger and feelings of depression and apathy were being replaced by cautious hope. Internal tensions resurfaced, resulting in nasty and often violent arguments, and replacing resignation and inertia. Theft was on the increase. We carried our precious Red Cross parcels tied to our belts, never letting them out of sight. At night we cradled them against our bodies, like newborn babies.

For starving prisoners, the bartering system assumed an importance out of all proportions to its merits. Every item of food had its established value. The bartering would start after the issue of the soup and bread – so many slices of bread for a bowl of soup, so many potatoes for bread, etc. Even the small amounts of cheese and margarine which were occasionally added to our rations, had an established value. When the parcels arrived, it was the first time that new, additional items entered the equation. The bartering started straight away. I managed to strike a bargain with a kitchen worker, a heavy smoker, who pinched the potatoes from the food store. Two potatoes for a cigarette was a good deal; for me it meant twenty days of extra food. For fifteen days I enjoyed the luxury of additional nourishment, then somebody stole my remaining five cigarettes. For me this was a disaster; it meant the loss of ten potatoes.

The issue of cigarettes turned out to be a mixed blessing. The non-smokers gained, the smokers lost. In one or two days they finished their cigarettes. This only served to increase their craving. They were prepared to go to any lengths to satisfy their addiction. They resorted to stealing, and a minority went so far as to trade in their food rations for cigarettes. In the unforgiving conditions of camp life, this usually meant joining the ranks of the Musselmänner.

Return to Camp No. 1

At the end of the winter, 1944-45, we were taken back to Camp No. 1. Before entering the camp we had to go through a new Entlausung – a shed for delousing. As we were undressing to go into the showers, we were instructed to leave our clothes in the heat chamber. Every item had to be laid out separately, to ease the heat penetration. As I was taking off my foot-wrappers, I suddenly realised that I could be in serious trouble. In Camp No. 3, I had felt safe enough to cut off bits from my blanket to make warm foot-wrappers for the winter. Now, however, I was in the domain of 'Napoleon' Kirsch, where five prisoners had been hanged for 'destroying state property'. I folded the wrappers and pushed them into the sleeves of my coat, hoping that nobody would discover the hiding place.

While we were enjoying our first hot shower for many years, the door opened and a very young SS man stepped into the room. Two prisoners followed, each holding a coat and a pair of foot-wrappers. The SS took one of the coats and called out for prisoner No. 82336 to step forward. I moved forward and stood to attention on legs trembling with fear. I had no choice, the prisoner number was printed on a tag attached to the coat. He then called out the number of the other coat and I was joined by a small, middle-aged man. The SS man continued, "To serve as a deterrent, you will now run through the Entlausung waving the foot-wrappers and shouting 'I am guilty of trying to hide these items, and my punishment will be twelve lashes.'" I nearly collapsed with relief. When we had finished our run through the lines of queueing prisoners and returned to the shower room, things looked grim. The naked men were lined up in a semi-circle; in the middle stood the SS man and a prisoner holding a whip. The middle-aged man was told to bend down and the first blow landed on his bare behind. The result was as sudden as it was unexpected; a mass of brown stools gushed out with some force and landed at the feet of the SS man. We watched in deathly silence as his right hand twitched towards his pistol. Then, as the foul smell began to spread, he issued orders to clean up and carry on the punishment, and then quickly made his exit.

Trembling like a leaf, the middle-aged man cleared up the mess and then took the twelve lashes without flinching. When my turn came, the feeling of nervous tension drowned out the physical pain. It was painful afterwards, but a few scars on the buttocks were better than a rope round the neck.

The Last Days of Camp No. 1

As we entered the camp, we received some good news: Kommando Lingemann was to be revived and all of us were going back to our previous plumbing jobs. The bad news followed later; I found Uncle Mike in the clinic, looking ill and emaciated. He gave me a long list of friends and acquaintances who had died of the spotted fever epidemic. Then I met Josh, a close friend of mine who had worked with me at Kaunas airport and then at the Heeresbau. He explained that although the epidemic took many lives, the quarantine was of considerable benefit. The inmates received the same rations and Red Cross parcels as the other camps, but did not have to work. He also told me that the new Entlausung had eliminated the scourge of lice. This was a change indeed; our main leisure time activity – dealing with the tiny bloodsuckers – was thus at an end.

However, the most amazing information was that five

Hungarian women had given birth in the camp hospital and had been allowed to keep the babies. It seemed to me like a minor miracle when, six months later, I discovered that mothers and infants had survived the liquidation of the camp and been liberated by the American army. The camp was full of new prisoners. Jews from Hungary, Poland, Greece and Czechoslovakia were continuously arriving from various concentration camps to replace the people lost by the epidemic and the atrocious working conditions.

A few days after my arrival at Camp No. 1, I had an encounter with a Polish Jew which brought home to me the horrors of Auschwitz even more forcefully than the accounts of the Hungarian women. He was part of a five-man crew of Greek and Polish Jews running the Entlausung. I knew from Josh's disclosures that all of them, including their boss, the young SS man, were evacuees from Auschwitz. Their work was clean and warm; they also had job security – the SS man rejected all attempts by the kapos to impose their own workers.

Our conversation did not start off well, "Are you one of those whinging Litvaks (Yiddish expression for Lithuanian) who don't realise how well off they are? Compared with Auschwitz, this is a holiday camp." I tried to assure him that we knew all about the hell of Auschwitz from the Hungarian women's accounts, but he got more agitated and aggressive. He described my comparison with hell as absurd and made the point that the purpose of hell was to punish the guilty, but the purpose of Auschwitz was to punish the innocent. When he noticed that I was startled by his statement, he quietened down and began to relate his experiences. It was a short, terse account which chilled my blood and disclosed the cause of his stressful behaviour.

Like many Polish Jews of the Lodz ghetto, he had finished up in Auschwitz. It was mid-1944, the year the Nazis decided to exploit the Jews for labour instead of exterminating them. He was a fit-looking man and was allocated to the so-called Sonderkommando (Special commando) which had the most harrowing of all the concentration camp jobs. They were the first to enter the gas chambers in order to prise apart and remove the tightly packed bodies, which were covered in sweat, blood and excrement as a result of their slow, agonising death. Then, under the close supervision of the brutal SS and Ukrainian guards, they had to search the corpses for hidden valuables and check every one for gold teeth. After the items they found and the extracted gold teeth were handed over to the guards, they took the bodies for cremation.

As he was telling his story, he was again getting agitated, his speech became hesitant, but he seemed determined to continue. He began to talk about the 'selections', a traumatic event which every arrival had to undergo and which determined who should live and who should die. Anybody who looked too frail or too old for work was doomed. For any woman, no matter how strong and healthy, to be accompanied by a child meant a death sentence. Consequently a large number of the victims were mothers and their children. Amongst them were his wife and their two daughters.

At this point his hesitant delivery ground to a halt. I felt there was a lot more he wanted to get off his chest, but he was too distraught to continue and left without a further word. When I saw him again, he looked gloomy and depressed and hardly acknowledged my greeting. Yet physically he was in good shape and his chances of survival were as good as anybody's. As to his state of mind, I feared that sooner or later the ghosts of Auschwitz might catch up with him.

We received another, larger Red Cross parcel. There was a tin of condensed milk as well as sugar and cigarettes. It was again a big help to me. The cigarettes meant extra bread or extra potatoes.

The work at Lingemann was not too demanding. There was no night shift, and some of the plumbing was done indoors. The chief was a corrupt and unpleasant civilian who diverted labour and materials to build himself a summer cottage. Our two supervisors were badly disabled ex-front line soldiers. Gestätter, a Bavarian, who had lost his toes through frostbite on the eastern front, was a narrow-minded, patriotic German. Schröder, wounded in the head and blind in one eye, was a Berliner, openly contemptuous of the Nazi leadership. He singled me out for storekeeping. I worked behind a counter, issuing tools and materials, reading German newspapers and witnessing the heated arguments between Gestätter and Schröder. This restful job helped me to recover from the ordeals of winter and gave me the strength to survive what was about to come.

The 'March'

The orders for the evacuation of the camp came on 24 April 1945. Except for the prisoners in the clinic, everybody had to collect their rations and assemble on the central square. The mood was one of uncertainty and confusion. We knew that the Russians had occupied Vienna and were at the outskirts of Berlin, and that the Americans were closing in fast. We were pretty sure that the Nazis' intention was to liquidate us. However, with the Americans only days away, it was not easy to arrange the slaughter of thousands of prisoners, and it was impossible to hide the evidence.

Josh and I each took a blanket and joined the columns, each of 100 men, for the march to Dachau. At the last minute we were joined by some sick people from the clinic and by some Musselmänner, who had no chance of surviving the journey. Uncle Mike stayed behind in the clinic. We walked all day and had to spend the night in the open, in cold and wet surroundings. The Musselmänner and the sick could not keep up with us. They kept collapsing and begged to be taken back to the camp. They were collected in groups, and guards were detached from the main body to stay behind with them. This was a good omen, as in the past they would have been shot. On the second day, as we were nearing Dachau, we noticed two Swiss Red Cross vans which seemed to follow us at a distance. We did not know exactly what it meant, but it was an encouraging sight.

It was dark when we entered Dachau, the oldest and largest concentration camp in Germany. Thousands of prisoners of various nationalities were milling around. We were cold, hungry and tired, and the ration of hot soup and bread revived us a bit.

After a short rest, we decided that it was vital to replace one of our wet and torn blankets. Because of the cold spring weather, Josh and I shared our two blankets. We used one as a cover, and the other one as a groundsheet. After just one night on wet grass, it became useless. We soon found a blanket warehouse which was under quarantine and carefully locked up. It was not guarded, but there were signs warning people to keep out because of the risk of spotted fever infection. To us it was no deterrent; having survived the epidemic, we were sure of our immunity. We broke in through a window, took a warm, heavy blanket and settled down for the night.

Liberation

In the morning we had to decide whether to follow orders and join our march, or to stay behind and hide amongst the thousands of prisoners. I did not feel strong enough to go on and thought of staying behind, but Josh regarded Dachau as a trap, a dangerous place, from which there was no escape in case of an emergency.

We joined the march and started out southwards towards the Bavarian mountains and lakes. We always slept in the open, sometimes during the day, sometimes during the night. The guards were a motley crew, mostly middle-aged or elderly soldiers of various nationalities. We had some emergency rations, but they only lasted a day. After skirting round the suburbs of Munich, we reached the open countryside with small villages and farms. Driven by hunger, I managed to sneak into a pig farm and pinch some swill from a pig trough. Despite the sour taste I swallowed it, but felt nauseous afterwards. After a couple of days, Josh and I started itching. We realised at once that it came from the blanket, but it never occurred to us to get rid of it.

The march was getting slower every day, and the rest intervals were increasing. We were moving along like sleep-walkers, unaware of time or surroundings. During a rest break, an elderly guard informed me that it was Sunday 30 April, and that the Americans were only a few miles away. The next day, when we noticed that the guards were unusually nervous and agitated, Josh and I decided that it was a sign that the Americans were near. In the evening, when we stopped near a wooded area, we sneaked deeper into the woods until we reached a good hiding place – a ditch behind some bushes. As soon as we put the blanket down, we noticed that the hollow was soggy, but we were too tired to do anything about it. We collapsed into a deep sleep of exhaustion.

It was light when I woke up. I felt cold and stiff and Josh had to help me up and pull me out of the ditch. Our blanket and clothing were wet from the melting snow which was lying in the hollow. We had to get out into the sun and dry out. We looked out from behind the bushes; everything seemed to be quiet and peaceful. A few figures in striped prison uniforms moved around near the road, and there was no sign of our guards. Reassured, we left our hiding place. The first prisoner we met was a Russian, one of a number of POWs who had joined our march a few days before. He told us that the guards had fled during the night and that everybody was hoping for the speedy arrival of the Americans. It was a sunny morning with good visibility; the prisoners were gathered on the road staring into the distance. Suddenly we heard a dull rumble and then a column of vehicles appeared on the horizon. Fearing it might be a retreating German unit, we cleared the road. Then somebody shouted, "The French are here!" Sure enough, the lead vehicle was flying the tricolour.

The column slowed down and the soldiers looked with amazement at the emaciated figures crowding round them. Now we knew for sure: we were free, this was the end of the long nightmare. I looked up at the smiling face of the driver of a military van. I was choking, and it took me a long time to recover my senses. It was the feeling of intense hunger which brought me back to reality, and my first words as a free man were a down-to-earth request for food, "Du pain, s'il vous plaît."

One year after liberation. Munich 1946

1947 in Munich on my way to ORT

I trained in radio engineering (standing left) Munich 1948

Our wedding day. August 1946

Happier days, with Ibi, Munich 1948 before our departure for England. The past behind us, but never far away.

116

With my wife, Ibi, after fifty two years of marriage

Our granddaughter, Amy

CHAPTER SIX

THE HIGH PRICE OF FREEDOM

LIBERATION AND BEYOND

Painful Awakening

The liberation took place on 1 May 1945, between Buchberg and Wolfratshausen, near the eastern shore of Lake Starnberg. We had walked for six days, covering about 95 miles, most of it on an empty stomach, but the effects of malnutrition reached way back, to the beginning of our imprisonment. Throughout the years, to exorcise the all-pervasive craving for food, we were constantly talking and dreaming about it. Now that we were in an American-run rest home, we could indulge our obsession. We ate enormous amounts of food without a rest and without feeling full. The dangers of overeating were only realised when the liberated prisoners began to die. Josh and I were no exception. Our weakened bodies could not cope with the excess food and we became ill with diarrhoea and bouts of vomiting. However, we recovered and by the end of the second week after liberation, we were well enough to be moved from the rest home in Bad Tolz to a Jewish centre for 'Displaced Persons' in Munich.

Confident that all our troubles were finally over, we were riding high on a wave of liberation euphoria and began making plans for our future. Meanwhile, the incubation time bomb was ticking away, ready to strike. We both fell ill at the same time. Josh was moved to an isolation hospital with suspected spotted fever, and I was transferred to the monastery of St Ottilien, between Munich and Landsberg, which had been converted into a military hospital.

The diagnosis took a while to emerge. As my condition deteriorated and I could not walk or use my hands, the doctors established that I was suffering from exhaustion and polyneuritis, brought on by sleeping in wet surroundings during the march. By that time liberation euphoria had come to an end. I was lying in a gloomy hospital ward in the care of dedicated doctors who did their best to heal the damages to mind and body of the concentration camp victims. The death rate was high despite all their efforts. To lose people who had survived the massacres and deprivations of the camps and stood on the threshold of a new, free life was especially upsetting. It was a severe blow when I found out that Uncle Mike, the only survivor of the large Garson family, had died two days after liberation. More depressing news soon followed: Josh had died of spotted fever.

Amidst all the gloom, there appeared a ray of hope which gave me some reason for cautious optimism: persistent rumours began to spread that Lithuanian women were liberated from Stutthof and that some of them were heading for Munich. The news of their imminent arrival at St Ottilien raised the excitement to fever pitch. One morning, quite unexpectedly, they walked into my ward, amongst them a few familiar faces from the Heeresbau and the concentration camp of Sanciai. As they approached my bed, I knew from their expressions that I must expect the worst, that I must prepare myself for a severe shock.

Tragedy at Sea

They told me the story in rough outline only, sparing me the details. Stutthof, like Dachau, had a lot of satellite slave labour camps. The women from Kaunas-Sanciai were in one of them, building a line of fortifications to impede the Russian advance. The back-breaking work continued throughout the winter, exacting a frightful toll. Anybody unable to keep up was taken to the crematorium of the main camp. At the end of April, as the Russians approached, the surviving women – including my mother – were taken to a Baltic port and loaded on ships. As they reached the open sea, Allied planes machine-gunned them and set one ship on fire. The guards started throwing the dead and wounded overboard. A young woman next to my mother was hit in the leg and was writhing in agony. As the guard, a brutal SS man, tried to throw her into the sea, my mother intervened, begging him to spare her. He declared that he was going to show all of them how to get rid of troublemakers. In front of the horrified prisoners, he let go of the wounded woman and threw my mother overboard. A few days later, the ships arrived in the Baltic port of Kiel, which was in the hands of the advancing British army, and all the survivors were freed.

More depressing stories followed about the final massacres of the Jews of the Kaunas ghetto, who were trying to hide in underground bunkers or conceal themselves behind false walls. After the deportations from Kaunas, between 8-12 July, the Nazis discovered from their records that a number of Jews must still be hiding in the ghetto. On 13 July, the Einsatzkommandos (Extermination squads), including Latvian militia, entered the remains of the reduced ghetto with machine-guns, petrol and explosives. The wooden buildings were drenched in petrol and set on fire; the larger apartment blocks were blown up with dynamite. Anybody hiding inside had two choices: to burn to death or to run and die in a hail of bullets. This went on for three days, until the ghetto was reduced to a smouldering wasteland with charred and bullet-ridden bodies lying all around. Only three underground bunkers remained undiscovered.

On 1 August, the Russians entered Kaunas and liberated the survivors of two bunkers. The inmates of the third were trapped and suffocated when the debris of the demolition cut off their supply of air. We were glad to get the list of names of the survivors, but it was dwarfed by the list of victims, amongst them the names of friends, relations and acquaintances.

The shock of these revelations added to my depression and plunged me into the nightmares of the past. I was not the only one to experience this reaction to past horrors. The physical and mental after-effects were sometimes immediate, sometimes delayed for a long time. They affected the survivors in different ways and to a different extent, but they were unavoidable. This reaction hit me earlier than the others, mainly because of the news of my mother's death and my debilitating illness. While the other survivors were busy rushing around, I was confined to bed, hardly able to move, feeling lonely and isolated from life outside.

All my time was taken up by introspective brooding. The moral contradictions of my existence on the brink of anni-hilation were tormenting me. I was assailed by feelings of guilt for having survived and for having felt relief at being spared, while around me my loved ones perished. Directing my thoughts to the carefree years of my pre-war life did little to lift my gloom. I felt shame at my failure to appreciate fully the love and devotion of my mother and family. I regretted that, owing to my attitude of benign indifference towards matters concerning family history, roots and experiences, there were large gaps in my recol-lections which could never be filled.

The grief I felt at the loss of my mother made me rancorous. I could not tolerate the presence of the liberated Stutthof women – the bearers of the devastating news of my loss. It seemed to me that the least deserving people had survived.

I felt that I must try to make sense of past events, but the more I delved into the past, the more my incomprehension deepened. My thoughts returned to the 'actions' of autumn 1941 when, engulfed by the terror, we were attempting to find answers to many questions. What happened to the empathy between people which used to be the bedrock of our beliefs? Did the outbreak of violence and aggression indicate that our belief in a benevolent and progressive humanity was just wishful thinking? Was it possible to explain why ordinary well-meaning people, who had lived in peace with their Jewish neighbours, turned against them and even participated in the atrocities?

I was also trying to recall my stepfather Samuel's arguments and reasoning which had seemed esoteric and remote, but had now acquired a new relevance. One of the questions I had frequently discussed with him in the early days of the pogroms was whether people's violent and aggressive behaviour was due to genetic factors or to external conditioning. Samuel did not believe in an innate aggressive drive and argued that it was irrationality and gullibility which made it easy to manipulate and indoctrinate people. I remembered his warning that the pre-war obsession with exclusivist ideologies, combined with human naïvety, would have dire consequences. He supported his warning about the danger of ideologies by pointing out that all of them, whether religious or secular, claim exclusive knowledge of the truth and the monopoly of all moral values. These claims reinforce the 'us' and 'them' divisions of society and breed fanatical believers who consider anyone outside their belief system as so morally wicked that he deserves to be eliminated.

After four years of imprisonment and three months of freedom, it seemed to me that I was again in prison, locked in by my painful immobility and stressful memories and by my obsession with the same old questions. My nights were spent fighting off my nightmares and my days feeling sorry for myself, grieving over the loss of my family and community. I brooded on Samuel's warning about the dangers of man's gullibility and propensity for violence, but whilst I was confused about the causes of human violence and aggression, I had few doubts about its consequences. Our bloody history was proof that the cycle of violence is unbreakable, that it never fails to return and shock us with new and more terrifying brutalities. The scale and scope of the excesses made me believe that the whole human species was like a malignant force, bent on destroying everything in its path, including its own kind.

Later, as events took a more positive turn, I came to feel that this view of humanity as a destructive force was too simplistic and inadequate, and did not take account of the complexity of human nature.

Recovery

I needed someone or something to help me to snap out of this obsession with the past. The doctors kept assuring me that my disease was not easy to cure, but a proper diet and an intensive vitamin B treatment would eventually restore my health. I remained pessimistic. Then, after three months of illness, I realised that the doctors were right. Slowly the reflexes in my legs and arms came back; I started moving around and, by the end of the fourth month, I could walk unaided. It took some time to recover fully, but my mood had changed, my confidence was restored.

Upper Bavaria had become a centre for the Jewish survivors of Lithuania. They kept trickling in from various parts of Germany, from Poland and the Baltic States, bringing with them vital information and news. As the lists of survivors were prepared, the extent of our losses became clear – over 90 per cent of the Jews of Lithuania had perished during the four years of the Nazi occupation.

It seemed to me that the centuries-old Jewish presence in Lithuania was at an end and there was nothing and nobody left to return home to. The accounts of some new arrivals, refugees from the Lithuanian Soviet Socialist Republic (LSSR), strengthened my impression. They were amongst the Jews liberated from their hiding place by the Red Army in August 1944. The liberation euphoria did not last long. They found it so difficult to start a new life that they risked life and limb to escape from the blood-soaked soil of their homeland.

The newcomers also brought some very cheerful news. My cousin Irena, who had left the ghetto to hide amongst Lithuanian friends, managed to survive despite some very close shaves. So did my cousins Margaret and Alick, the children of George Strom. The other event which cheered me up was the arrival of a handful of Jewish children, hidden and cared for by Lithuanians, who were trying to restore them to their rightful parents. Some children were reunited with members of their families; some discovered that they were orphans.

One of the Lithuanian families who had saved the life of a little boy, the son of a Jewish doctor, stayed for a few months in St Ottilien. They received VIP treatment from the grateful father who was chief doctor of the hospital, and they made a good recovery from the ordeal of their flight from Kaunas and their hazardous trek through Germany.

I was keen to talk to them to find out about life on the other side of the prison fence and also to discover the special attributes of people who were prepared to risk their own and their family's lives in order to save Jewish children. Many were ordinary people, without any special religious or other convictions, and their explanation for their altruism was just as ordinary. "It was the right thing to do at the time; we just had to help a friend in trouble."

I got most of my information from Jonas, the youngest member of the family. Some of it, relating to the pre-war views and attitudes of the Lithuanian population, was so unexpected that it challenged many of my beliefs. My notion that the support of Jews for the independence struggle and their contributions to the country's economy had removed most of the old antisemitic prejudices, was, it seems, never true.

Jonas argued that the multicultural, polyglot nature of Kaunas which I described in such glowing terms in the section 'Varieties of Life' was resented by the Lithuanian population. It made them feel threatened and isolated, especially since the re-emergence of their culture and autonomy was still in embryonic stage. Jewish cultural autonomy was even more disliked; it was regarded as unpatriotic and a rejection of native culture. However, in spite of Jonas' awareness of divisions within society and their potential for conflict, he had shared my belief that pogroms could never happen on Lithuanian soil.

He was a little older than I was, but in many respects our pre-war life was very similar. He had also led a sheltered and carefree life; his family belonged to the 'capitalist class'. Their property was also confiscated by the Soviet authorities and, like us, they were saved from deportation to Siberia by the German invasion. That is where our paths diverged. While we were plunged into the nightmare of the pogroms, his life returned to near normal. The Germans even restored some confiscated property. For a while, the new occupiers were considered as liberators from Communist oppression and were very popular.

However, Jonas soon became aware that for one group of people, there was no return to near-normal conditions. To them the normal codes of morality did not apply. The antisemitic hate propaganda became more vicious than ever, maintaining that the disaster of Soviet occupation was the work of the Jews. But what dismayed him even more was the fact that it was disseminated by the official Lithuanian press and radio, and that it was placing the whole Jewish community beyond the pale.

When he first heard about the pogroms, he assumed that they were isolated deeds by lawless groups. However, he soon realised that large sections of the population had succumbed to the brainwashing; and when the partisans started organising the shooting of Jews and plunder of their property, they were joined not only by the misfits of society, but also by otherwise decent and law-abiding citizens.

Jonas also became aware that the true aims of the German 'liberators' were to exploit and colonise Lithuania. The arrival of German settlers, the round-up of able-bodied men for forced labour and conscription, the arrest of Lithuanian leaders who refused to go along with the occupier's plans, convinced him that he should leave Kaunas and go to stay with his relatives in the countryside. And yet, despite this antagonistic atmosphere, when the Red Army was poised to overrun Lithuania in summer 1944, the whole family unanimously decided to flee west. They preferred to live as refugees in war-ravaged Germany rather than face the near certainty of deportation to a Siberian labour camp.

After my recovery, I decided to stay for a while in the pleasant surroundings of St Ottilien, which meant that I had to get a temporary job. That was not very difficult: I knew the hospital administrators well; they were mainly Lithuanian Jews, the same privileged minority who had had the cushy jobs in the ghetto, then in the concentration camps. My job as a security man left me plenty of time to have a good look at the world around me, to start planning my future and find out about educational opportunities.

My next step was a trip to Munich, the centre of the Jewish Committee for 'Displaced Persons', to consult them about the activities of ORT, the school for vocational training. A crash course in radio engineering was due to commence in January 1946, and I decided to join it. I was surprised to see the extent of the bomb damage in Munich. Whole quarters of the town were razed to the ground. There was rubble everywhere; the population looked harassed and miserable. Refugees from the eastern German territories, who were escaping from the murder, rape and pillage of the Red Army, were flooding into Bavaria.

Germany was ruined, and in an economy in chaos it was the black market which reigned supreme. The liberated concentration camp prisoners were intensely disliked. They were blamed for organising the black market and for other ills affecting the country. My impression was that despite denials, the people were aware of the mass murder of Jews and other atrocities committed by the Nazis in the name of Germany, but they were still in a state of shock and in no position to confront their guilt. They preferred to find solace in self-induced amnesia and were just as eager as camp survivors to wipe out the traumatic memories of the past and concentrate on rebuilding their shattered lives.

While working in St Ottilien, I became friendly with a Hungarian girl called Ibi, a survivor of Auschwitz who came to Camp No. 1 in the autumn of 1944 with one of the transports of Jewish women. She was a native of Tokaj, a wine-growing region in the north-east of Hungary. Her ordeal had started in the spring of 1944, when the Nazis became dissatisfied with Hungary's lukewarm commitment to the war effort and lenient attitude towards the Jews. The Germans occupied the country and on 19 March 1944, Adolf Eichmann was installed in Budapest to organise the liquidation of the Hungarian Jews. Ibi and her family – her mother, father and three younger sisters – were imprisoned in a ghetto near Tokaj for about four weeks and then at the end of May, taken to Auschwitz.

Ibi told me about the circumstances surrounding her experiences. The Jews, who were already dismayed and bewildered by the sudden change in their circumstances, became even more alarmed by the sight of the watchtowers, barbed wire, armed guards with vicious dogs straining at the leash, and the all-pervasive smell of burning flesh. However, there was no panic; Nazi assurances that the deportations were needed to alleviate labour shortages throughout Germany were firmly believed, and any talk or rumours to the contrary were dismissed as absurd or malicious.

After disembarking from the cattle wagons, the men were separated from the women and children. The whole camp seemed full of noise and confusion. The SS men and prisoners in striped garb were rushing around; the dogs were growling and barking. Only one immaculately dressed man was calm and collected. He was scrutinising the women, sending the young and healthy-looking ones to one side and the elderly or sick-looking and all the children to the other. To prevent panic and help the deception, mothers were not parted from their children. Taking advantage of the general fracas, the veteran prisoners tried to whisper to them to leave the children with the grandmother or with the elderly women, but this advice was met with looks of resentment or incomprehension.

During the selection, Ibi and her sister Judith, who was 13 then but looked older, were separated from their mother and the two youngest sisters aged seven and ten. It was a worrying and confusing development but the true purpose of separation was not suspected. They had faith in the promise of the SS guards that they would be soon reunited. On leaving the selection site, they caught a glimpse of their father, marching in a column of men. Unlike his wife and two younger daughters, he survived his imprisonment in the concentration camp of Mauthausen and arrived in St Ottilien in February 1946 to be reunited with his two eldest daughters.

After a visit to the Entlausung for a clean up and for the removal of all body hair, the women were allocated to their barracks. It was not long before the true nature of Auschwitz began to be suspected, but it was a long time before it was believed. The rough hardened inmates were irritated by the refusal of the newcomers to face reality and pointed at the huge smoking chimneys, "That's the only way to leave the death camp!"

Three months later, when the Hungarian women entered our camp, the expression of horror was still imprinted on their faces. The day they arrived, it was pouring with rain and our commando was lined up not far from 'Napoleon' Kirsch, who was watching the wet and emaciated bundles of human misery stagger into the shelter of the kitchen barrack. I expected him to take charge and to start throwing his weight about, but instead he just stood still, rooted to the spot, silently staring at the women. There was an expression of bewilderment and embarrassment in his eyes. For me, it was one of those moments which are unforgettable by a sudden, unexpected insight. The same day he gave orders for the Hungarian newcomers to take over the cushy kitchen and sick-bay jobs hitherto held by the Lithuanian women. Yet it was the same man who, a couple of months later, ordered the hanging of 5 prisoners for damaging state property.

The friendship between Ibi and me was a turning point for both of us. Very soon we fell in love. It gave us new confidence and hope – confidence that together we could exorcise the events of the past, and hope that together we could face the future and build a new life.

We were married in the summer of 1946, moved to Munich and settled down to the routine of our new life. I finished my studies and was fortunate to get a good job. I became an instructor at ORT and kept the position until our departure to England in the autumn of 1948, where we eventually settled in Elland, West Yorkshire. Today, our two daughters and three grandchildren are a constant source of joy to us. At one time we thought we had no future. Now, to see our grandchildren growing and learning and enjoying life, is the most positive gift we could hope for, as they are our future. I have written down my experiences for them and for their generation.

IN CONCLUSION

I have tried to tell you my story as simply as I know how. You must be aware that I have only attempted to deliver a documentary statement of fact as it seems impossible to convey the real feelings of these terrifying days. I would be bold enough to suggest that language itself could not relate either the devastating fear nor the surreal normality of what we went through. At one moment you witnessed murder and bloodshed, screaming and sobbing, the next you were plumbing. One day you were with your family, the next you were totally alone. It is difficult to describe what this does and how you feel, because strangely, although you are at the extreme of human existence, somehow you continue to live through it.

There is also a strange irony about these days, as it appears the worse the evil that is perpetrated, the more difficult it is to explain or understand. For example, in one sentence I mentioned that of the fourteen members of my family who met to decide what to do in advance of the German invasion, only I survived. What that means, is that fourteen members of my immediate family were murdered. I do not know if you have had opportunity to meet the family of a murder victim before, but if you have, you will be aware of the impact such a tragedy has on their lives. Each could tell their own story. Now try to imagine having your whole family murdered. There were no accidents, just brutal and sometimes slow deaths. These were the people I loved. It is difficult to even know where to start to explain what that means.

There are now many accounts of the Holocaust years. Some are written by fellow victims of persecution like myself, others are by professional historians, researching and documenting a difficult, but important, period. My story will perhaps add one more perspective to the many that already exist.

In my native Kaunas, there now live very few Jews. Most were murdered during the Holocaust. Many of those who remain are now elderly and soon there will be virtually nothing left of the Jews of Kaunas. In a way, my testimony is given as my personal tribute to the community of people I lived with and belonged to. Most did not live to tell their own story, and so my words are in part written on their behalf. I hope that they will bear witness to their loss and remind future generations to think before they indulge in similar activities.